Praise for Financial Con1 Digital Agencies

This book is like a comprehensive meeting with an accountant who asks you all the questions you need to consider as an agency owner - some you've been asking yourself already, some you've been avoiding, and some you didn't even know to ask. It's both detailed and readable in relation to your finances. Ultimately (and rightly) it prioritises the impact your agency has on you, the owner and leader.
Karen L Reyburn, CPA, Owner of The Profitable Firm Ltd

As an agency founder, I've spoken of the difference in the maturity of digital agencies versus other professional services firms such as PR companies, and legal or accountancy practices. It took many years to arrive at a set of structures and processes where my agency became consistently profitable. The result was not only a successful exit, but perhaps more importantly a very happy team, very happy clients, and a very relaxed and enjoyable experience for me running the agency. This book provides a blueprint for exactly this scenario. For agency founders and leaders, this book is gold.
Steve Brennan Co-founder & CEO Bespoke Digital Agency

I first met Paul, and MAP, back in 2015 when having invested in a Digital Agency, I found the financial recording and reporting to be missing some key aspects. To put it bluntly I needed to

get more confidence in the numbers. Over the following years I worked with MAP to provide me with what I needed to gain Financial Confidence in my business. The lessons in this book come from 10 years of helping agency owners understand their finances that much better, building Financial Confidence in their businesses, and in many cases achieving better outcomes. If you need to learn how to use finance as a tool to get what you need from your business, then I can't recommend this book strongly enough.
Stuart Brown, Chairman, MAP. The Digital Agency Finance Function

The thing I love about this book is how it challenges you on why you're running an agency. It's a blueprint not just for a financially sound and sustainable business, but one that provides fulfilment and rewards well beyond numbers on a spreadsheet.
Andrew Armitage, Founder of Digital agency A Digital

As an adviser to agency owners, I see a lot of different shapes and sizes but every single one is on a journey to their own goal. No matter where you are on yours, this book provides the insights and tools to accelerate your progress, guiding you toward achieving both your personal and professional goals. This book is your shortcut to a happier and healthier business.
Adam Downes FPFS Chartered Financial Planner, Pura Vida

A stimulating read for digi-agency owners looking to drive growth and scalability written from a hands-on, practical perspective of deep experience. Don't be fooled by its easy-to-read style though, as it will challenge you to really self-examine and consider your 'why' before giving you a roadmap for the 'how'. Get a copy for your entire leadership team and business book club.
Max Clark, Founder and Director, Upp B2B

FINANCIAL CONFIDENCE FOR DIGITAL AGENCIES

A framework for
building the business
you've always wanted

Paul Barnes

First published in Great Britain by Practical Inspiration Publishing, 2025

© Paul Barnes, 2025

The moral rights of the author have been asserted

ISBN   9781788606387   (hardback)
        9781788606394   (paperback)
        9781788606417   (epub)
        9781788606400   (mobi)

All rights reserved. This book, or any portion thereof, may not be reproduced without the express written permission of the author.

Every effort has been made to trace copyright holders and to obtain their permission for the use of copyright material. The publisher apologizes for any errors or omissions and would be grateful if notified of any corrections that should be incorporated in future reprints or editions of this book.

Want to bulk-buy copies of this book for your team and colleagues? We can customize the content and co-brand *Financial Confidence for Digital Agencies* to suit your business' needs.

Please email info@practicalinspiration.com for more details.

Practical Inspiration Publishing

MIX
Paper | Supporting responsible forestry
FSC® C013604

Dedication

To my family, for your unwavering encouragement and the sacrifices you made to allow me to follow my passion and build something meaningful.

To my colleagues, past and present, whose hard work and personal support have been invaluable throughout this journey. I will forever cherish the dedication and passion you've brought to me and MAP.

To our clients, whose trust and loyalty have been the foundation of everything I've built. Thank you for believing in me and in the work we do together.

To our suppliers and partners, for your collaboration and continued support, helping MAP grow and thrive.

And, finally, to my dad. You taught me the importance of hard work, but more importantly, you showed me the value of doing what truly fulfills you. Your encouragement to spend my time pursuing what I love is something I carry with me every day.

Contents

INTRODUCTION *xi*
   The definition of confidence *xii*

PART 1: THE DIGITAL AGENCY GROWTH CHALLENGE: DO YOU STILL WANT THIS? *1*

Chapter 1: Digital agencies are different *3*
   Do you still want this? *6*
   Coming to an informed decision *7*
   The key questions to ask from the data *8*
   Appetite to continue *9*
   Your decision to act *11*

Chapter 2: Is your finance function fit for purpose? *13*
   Glass ceiling *14*
   The technician's curse *16*
   Towards maturity *19*
   Financial maturity versus financial performance *19*

PART 2: THE FINANCE MATURITY CURVE 23

Chapter 3: Essentials: First steps in digital agency growth 25
Appropriate and effective data: The foundation for scalable financial processes 26
Compliance: Protecting your reputation through quality and timely delivery 29
Management accounts: Essentials: An accurate account of financial activity 41

Chapter 4: Enhanced: From numbers to narrative 47
Budget 47
Management accounts: advanced 55
Projections 59
Why and when to forecast cash flow 60
Enhanced: Bringing facts into the figures: Creating a budget for your digital agency – what not to overlook 67

Chapter 5: Extended: Mature financial thinking 75
Financial leadership 76
Mapping the strategy 84
Best and worst clients 92
Specialist services 96
Taking money and value out of your company 114
Research and development 145

PART 3: WELCOME TO FINANCIAL MATURITY 147

Chapter 6: Mapping strategy to figures 149
Client concentration 150
Lack of recurring revenue 150
Woolly proposition 151
Relying on expensive talent 151
Wrong shape and size 152
Distraction 152
Lack of process 152

Margin erosion *153*
Appropriate investment *153*

Chapter 7: Specialist services *155*

Chapter 8: What next? *161*
From ego to honesty *162*
The curious mind *163*
Growth versus fixed mindset *164*

Appendix 1: The MAP way *167*
Should I hire an FD? *168*
The finance partner *170*
Elevate your finance function *170*
Definitely NOT an FD *173*
Free consultation *174*

Appendix 2: List of useful tools and resources *175*

Appendix 3: References *177*

Index *179*

Introduction

WE LIVE IN a world as full of opportunity as it is distraction. Never has it been easier to set up a business, market your brand and deliver services at scale. There is an abundance of ideal clients that will benefit from the work you do. You have access to resources worldwide to help you to deliver first-class results. Software and artificial intelligence is available to streamline the mundane and improve both customer service and margin.

But with this abundance of opportunity also comes a busy and distracted mind, and many business owners are suffering from decision fatigue. Which team structure should we go with? Which marketing tactics should we deploy? How fast should we grow?

All this opportunity, without a plan, is just chaos. Having a curious mind can be good if used in the right way, but when you find yourself jumping from one idea to another, progress is halted and the business that you really want stays just out of reach. You will only get out of this cycle if you take the time to get clear on what you *really* want and build a plan that matters for you and your family.

If you have set up a business for any other reason than to give you and your family a better quality of life, then I hope you will use this as an opportunity to reflect on what really matters.

If you want to finally achieve clarity on what it is that you want from this business and confidence that you know how to achieve it, then read on.

The definition of confidence

Confidence: The feeling or belief that one can have faith in or rely on someone or something.[1]

Building a business is not a straight line. It is a rollercoaster of ups and downs, but those ups and downs can be smoothed out by getting clear on the direction of travel and aiming everything else towards it.

When you have a plan that you can believe in, you become instantly clearer on what you need to do (and not do). With that clarity, in turn, you gain confidence that you can achieve your own ambition. Your ambition is absolutely unique to you, but once you've defined it, the tools in this book will guide you towards it.

If you occasionally find yourself asking these questions, this book is for you:

- Are we using the best tools to manage our business and its finances?
- Are we being as efficient as we could be?
- Is the business structured effectively?
- Are we as profitable as we could be?
- Are we pricing properly?
- Are we making the most of the tax planning opportunities available to us?

---

[1] *www.lucidity.org.uk/whats-the-difference-between-confidence-and-resilience/#:~:text=Confidence%20is%20the%20feeling%20or%20belief%20that%20one%20can%20have%20faith%20in%20or%20rely%20on%20someone%20or%20something*

- Are we offering the most attractive perks to our team members?
- Do our customers pay us as quickly as they should?
- What are our blind spots?
- Are we missing out on growth opportunities that we have not thought of?

This book has been created from hundreds of agency owners asking me and the MAP team these questions. The MAP team has compiled their answers and developed them into a format that enables you to learn from this combined experience amassed over the last decade.

If you are looking for overnight success, I am afraid you are going to be disappointed with this book. Instead, it will require you to create the building blocks for long-term, sustainable growth. If you do that, you have a high chance of building a high-performing agency.

It's not that difficult; it just requires getting clear on what you want and following some best practice to help you get there.

I promise it will be worth it.

The business you always wanted is within reach and you are already one step closer by picking up this book. Let's continue the journey…

Part 1
The digital agency growth challenge: Do you still want this?

Chapter 1
Digital agencies are different

DIGITAL MARKETING WAS first used as a term in the 1990s (Appendix 3:1), as search engines came into our world and a digital revolution was about to begin. The digital transformation market is today valued in excess of $3.3 trillion (Appendix 3:2). It is still a relatively very young industry and one that needs work to mature.

In the early 2000s, if you had digital skills, you were automatically in demand and could charge well for your services. Today, the market is saturated and competition is fierce, meaning winning work is getting harder and prices are being driven down. The power has shifted from supplier to customer, leading to tighter deadlines despite increased expectations on quality and quantity of output. It is no wonder that leaders of digital agencies are feeling stressed and overworked amidst increased effort for diminished returns. These businesses are not doomed; they just need tightening up before it's too late.

Digital agencies exist because of their ability to think creatively and find innovative solutions for business problems. Businesses benefit from this external viewpoint – people bringing fresh thinking and ideas to their teams.

Externally, that is your place in the market and why customers come to you. Internally, that drive for creativity and innovation can cross the chasm from opportunity to significant risk, which if not managed properly can have catastrophic consequences.

I have seen too many digital agencies get spellbound by the latest market trends to the detriment of their core operations, that is, the thing that makes them money and keeps them in business. Research and development, innovation, think labs, whatever you want to call it, they have a place, but they must be circumvented to prevent them becoming cash drainers beyond what the agency's resources can weather.

Amidst all the advice of the value being in building products and avoiding 'selling time for money', most of the healthy agencies that I have known *are* essentially selling time (expertise) for money. Often they are in fact pure service businesses; they just got really good at doing it profitably.

When it comes to selling a business, all but one of the successful deals I have been involved in were for well-run service businesses. The thing they all had in common was that they knew how to make money on their people. They created a high-performance culture that rewarded their people fairly while charging their customers properly.

I fear that with the push for an 'easier' life, agency owners are giving up hope of building the kind of business they originally envisaged. Instead, they are seeking that unicorn idea that has customers subscribing to their clever piece of software in their masses. They have been told about the hockey curve and that they need to spend their way through to the holy grail of a scalable

Software as a Service (SAAS) model. Yet, staggeringly, 80% of SAAS businesses fail in their first five years (Appendix 3:3).

Obviously, if you do find a new untapped opportunity to scale a SAAS business, great! I did it myself with software in the accounting sector. Like many business ideas, it came about as an accident as we built some tech to help our accounting firm to build proposals face to face with our customers. Essentially, it put the customer in control and we facilitated a buying environment for them to procure our services through our software, increasing conversion rates and basket value, while reducing the sales cycle. Brilliant!

We quickly realized that other accountants would love to create the same experience for their customers and so we spun it out as a standalone business, scaled to 1,500 subscribers and sold it to a FTSE Public Listed Company (PLC) less than four years later.

It was a great success story and secured my family's financial freedom.

But during that journey into SAAS, the accountancy firm continued to deliver healthy financial returns. We didn't allow our attention for running a well-oiled service business to be distracted. We had two very different business models running parallel and we recognized them as that. Separate leadership teams, Board meetings and offices. We could flick between one business and the other because we kept them separate.

If the SAAS business had failed, we still had our service business motoring along perfectly well. We could afford to fail. We also avoided the hockey curve. Instead of spending our way to a capital event (the exit), we got there through four years of healthy profitability. We never borrowed any cash and injected very little of our own. We built a basic version of the technology at low cost, incubated it in our own accountancy firm and my co-founder was gifted with an ability (and worked incredibly hard) to create compelling marketing content and push it out organically.

It would have been easy to get distracted by the more scalable SAAS business. People say that service businesses are harder work. It depends how you look at it but try asking the 80% of SAAS businesses that fail in their first five years that I mentioned earlier (Appendix 3:3). The SAAS sector has more extreme failures and successes. Service businesses might be harder to scale but they are usually easier to make profitable.

Digital agencies are service businesses cursed with the constant pull of building products. This book shows you how to run a high-performing digital agency service business, regardless of whether you build another business alongside it.

If you have lost some of your faith in the ability to build a successful business, think about these two things: firstly, many others are managing to achieve it, and secondly, you are likely to be much closer than you think.

Do you still want this?

Before you commit to the hard work involved in building a high-performing agency, I first want to check that this is definitely still for you. This book will help you to put the pieces together for a robust and profitable agency, if that's what you want. The first step to financial maturity and confidence though is getting clear on what you actually want from life. As the agency sector has become saturated with competition and large businesses are learning how to build in-house capability, it is becoming unquestionably more challenging to succeed.

The question now, especially for those who have been able to build good businesses and healthy balance sheets in recent years, is whether or not to capitalize on this good run and do something different, or to go again.

When you've been so wrapped up in building a business, it can be very difficult to take a step back and consider whether it is still serving the personal purpose that you originally intended. I have worked with several agency owners who decided to close the doors, get their cash out of the business and start a new chapter.

So, how do you work out whether this agency is still right for you?

Coming to an informed decision

Not all the components are going to be hard facts. Indeed, some of the most critical will rely on emotional and deeply personal responses, so it's worth breaking down to ensure the two are separated out as much as possible:

- Business dynamics, and the financial health of the agency.
- Scenarios – understanding the steps that can be taken and their financial impact.
- Self-reflection – your personal motivation and response.

The situation many find themselves in

The passion to turn around a struggling business can often get in the way of you doing the right thing for you and your family.

It is important to recognize that a struggling business is often not a reflection on you, your team or the quality of your clients and work, but the market reality impacting many other businesses in your sector.

As an agency owner, the business can often be a big part of your life, and economic downturns can be a sudden shock to the system. Good work that has been done over many years has been fundamentally put at risk overnight by something outside of your control. If the business has had good years in the past and built good reserves, watching this potentially eroding away can be a difficult thing to face.

Other factors may come into play, such as how well staff have stepped up to provide support and leadership, gaining an accurate view of client intentions and whether it is wise to invest in potential new opportunities.

I have witnessed agency owners digging themselves deeper and deeper holes when instead they could have achieved a really positive outcome by taking stock and making a plan at an earlier stage.

The options

When market conditions are against you and the business is losing money, I encourage you to work through three scenarios to bring clarity and lead to an informed decision.

The list is not limitless, but finding the right version of the right answer will be specific to your situation:

1. **Stop:** Liquidate the agency and return as much capital to shareholders as possible.
2. **Exit:** Find a suitable and viable option to pass to others through sale or other means.
3. **Continue:** Bear any losses, capitalize on opportunities and plan for renewed growth.

If exiting the business is an option, you should also consider what you will do next and what capital may be required for your next venture.

The key questions to ask from the data

This book is focused on helping you to continue running your business with new vigour and focus. If your business is currently in survive mode, and you want to get back to thrive mode, there are some questions you need to ask yourself.

Figure 1.1. Business model questions

Costs

- Can we continue with a smaller, or more flexible, workforce?
- Can we make our costs more flexible, for example, freelancers as needed?
- Do we need to reinvest or double-down in any areas?

Services

- Pivot – is there another angle to what we are doing?
- Can we deploy existing 'in demand' services like ecommerce to a new client base?
- Should we stop some service lines completely?
- Would there be synergies joining forces with another agency?

Motivations

- Do each of the shareholders want the same thing?
- How do you feel about continuing and what the future might hold?
- Do you have the right team around you to provide leadership and support?

Appetite to continue

Beyond the purely financial is how you are feeling about the challenges ahead.

We know that agency owners are driven by determination, but it might not be enjoyable or enough in itself to ensure you can make sufficient money. We also know that if you're not getting a break, just how stressful and disheartening it can be. A support team is what you need:

Having the support internally, and professionally, is important so that you are not facing the challenges ahead feeling as if everything relies upon you alone.

These are not signs of weakness or a lack of faith in what can be achieved, but recognition that you have a responsibility to look after your own mental health, preserving the success you have enjoyed so far and preparing for the next part of your journey.

Continue: planning for future growth

Given the passion that many agency owners have, your assessment could also underscore your desire and determination to continue – but perhaps with a renewed focus, a change in direction or a collaboration that can pull on relative strengths.

It's also worth considering what other operational changes could be made. Getting the essential data together can help reveal whether or not you have:

- Good financial controls
- Grip on costs
- Confidence in revenue
- Profitable business model

There also might be negotiations with suppliers that could have a material cash benefit, for example, with the landlord, suppliers and even staff dropping down to part-time.

And are there ways in which you can develop leaders within the team who can help guide and create buy-in for your plans – and reduce your stress? You should be looking for them to make decisions and not need your input all the time.

Thinking carefully about whether you have the right people in situ could prompt you to make a change that will transform how much is riding exclusively on your shoulders.

Your decision to act

The bravery and creativity to build an agency and have it play such an important part in your life can never be undervalued. It can be exhilarating, fun and stressful in equal measures – but you didn't start it for an easy life!

Being an entrepreneur is about knowing when to get out and play another game and when to make the changes to take things to another level. And regardless of the factors outside of your control, you get the right to choose to protect what you've built up – or cut your losses and exit to start a new chapter if that's what you want.

Make sure that you are supported in making the right decision for you – and that you are rewarded with the most value. If you are going to engage external help, choose someone who cares about the best outcome for you and be very alert to anyone trying to railroad you down a certain route.

Chapter 2
Is your finance function fit for purpose?

IMAGINE THE SCENARIO...
You walk into the boardroom for your regular monthly meeting. Your leadership team is alongside you and they are prepared and looking forward to the meeting. The agenda is laid out on the table, but you already know what's on there because it was circulated two days before the meeting. You take your seat and the chairperson opens the meeting by running through the actions set at the last meeting. As each action is read out, the relevant assignee responds with one word: 'Done.'

The chairperson moves the meeting on to the financial information. Again, everyone in the room has seen the reports in advance so the time is used to listen and respond to the questions that people have prepared in advance. The questions are discussed and concluded promptly and another month of meeting the financial targets is formally closed.

The remainder of the agenda follows with key strategic priorities discussed and issues resolved. New actions are set and assigned to the most appropriate person in the room, with due dates. The meeting finishes at the exact time agreed and everyone leaves the room feeling good and ready to go back into battle with a clear plan.

As the month progresses, the targets are clear to the whole company. Everyone knows what is being measured and how they contribute to the success of the overall business. The team loves achieving together. They encourage one another and make themselves available to anyone who would benefit from their support.

Clients are delighted with the service they are receiving. They trust in your business because they see that you are a transparent and caring partner. They couldn't imagine operating without you. The business is winning awards because not only is the service excellent, so too is the culture, the growth and the financial performance.

You are making more money than you ever believed you would. You are regularly receiving approaches to buy your business, but you have so much going well you feel like you could do this forever. If this sounds exciting to you, it's probably because you set up a business full of passion and belief that you could build something remarkable. If you are not yet experiencing this level of maturity and your business is not thriving the way that you want it to, chances are, you've hit a glass ceiling and you need a breakthrough.

Glass ceiling

Almost every agency hits a glass ceiling at some point. The growth previously experienced begins to plateau and progress becomes really difficult. This change doesn't happen overnight; it's a gradual process that eventually takes its toll on those running the business.

The more people you hire, the more complex the business becomes and if the processes and culture don't keep up, small cracks begin to expand.

The best agencies get proficient at identifying these issues and prioritizing them so that they can continue to grow in a sustainable way. And at the heart of every successful business is a reliable and insightful finance function. One that provides operational control and strategic input. Having access to the right information at the right time is crucial but unless that information is then used to inform and support planning, it is wasted time, cost and energy.

Unfortunately, finance is often the last to know about key business activities, finding out only when they process the transactions, which is too late for them to have added any value beyond data processing and compliance.

Those that see finance as a powerful resource available to input into business planning will bring finance into the heart of the business and include finance professionals in leadership meetings. Without proper attention to finance, you are sailing blindly into the ocean with no idea if you are on track to where you are heading or if you are about to hit an iceberg. Finance is the ultimate tool for illustrating the performance of your business. Warren Buffet calls it 'the language of business' (Appendix 3:4).

Unfortunately, most businesses don't give finance the respect it needs. They think business is about making sales and delivering a good service. The reality is that many businesses that have looked good from the outside have sadly failed because of weak financial controls. There are agencies twice the size of yours making less money. Conversely, there are others that are half the size yet making more.

You can run a small lifestyle agency that makes lots of money and you love working in it. You can run a much bigger agency that also makes good money and runs without you. There is no right and wrong here, just different preferences. Both are perfectly good options because they mean you are not burning yourself out with survival as the only goal.

Instead, I want your goal to be to build a thriving business that makes you proud and happy. I want your finance function to be insightful and reliable, not like a handbrake holding you back. If you struggle to get meaningful and actionable financial information that you can rely upon, you will never be able to build a high-performing agency.

You will get away with it in the early days of starting up a business. At that stage it's mainly about 'founder's hustle' – the passionate business owner pushing their proposition to everyone they speak to. Most of your energy and resources here should be spent on getting sales in. Overheads are low, and understanding the numbers is simple. So many businesses fail at this stage because of a lack of market traction.

If you achieve that traction and get revenue from paying customers funding the startup phase of the business, you can often get through without any external debt and probably without putting much of your own money at risk. It's not like a technology business that has to fund the development of a platform before it can seek customers. A service business has skill and expertise available to sell from day one.

The technician's curse

Many business experts will talk about the risks of starting a business in your area of expertise or craft; you are more likely to get sucked into operations and struggle with delegation because your clients want to work with you directly and you know you can provide a great service. One of the counter arguments to this concern though is that in those critical early days, you already have something to sell that doesn't cost anything other than your time.

It also helps to build a business on processes that you have tried, tested and even built yourself. It's much easier to know what to expect of others when you have been in their shoes.

As an owner–operator service business (where the majority shareholder also runs the business) grows, a number of challenges present themselves:

- You no longer have relationships with all the clients.
- You are not involved in all of the projects.
- You don't even manage all of the people that manage the clients and projects.

Ultimately, you become more removed from the operations, and so you should. This is an essential step to scaling a business and therefore doing so is testament to the success you have had so far. With this success, you need new ways of influencing the performance of the business. You are now no longer controlling delivery so you rely on data to inform your assessment and decision making. Data is the first step to prioritization and action.

Without this data you start to experience:

- Project overruns
- Scope creep
- Margin erosion
- Poor customer experience
- People performance issues
- Stagnant or declining revenues
- Customers paying late
- Paying too much tax

And many more other risks to your business.

Unfortunately, many business owners see this unfold and come to the conclusion that they no longer want to grow their business. The problems are getting bigger and the rewards are getting smaller. The juice just doesn't feel like it's worth the squeeze.

What is required in order to grow through this challenge is for the business to mature. You simply can't run it the way you always have and expect it to work out. Your role evolves from salesperson to Chief Executive Officer (CEO). Too many CEOs are still stuck in salesperson mode. They think the way to grow through all of their problems is to bring more sales in. Essentially, they are throwing more fuel into a broken engine. The small problems that they were hoping to extinguish in fact just become bigger problems.

Obviously, I want your business to mature so that you don't wind up in this vicious cycle. Instead, you can build a flourishing business on solid foundations. One that you want to grow because it gets more fun every time you win a new customer or a new team member instead of more stressful. Whether you have an appetite for scale or being small and mighty, with a mature business you have options and the freedom to choose. It's about having faith that what you are doing works. It's about financial confidence.

Businesses get held back by their finance function in a number of ways:

- **Diminished responsibility**: If there is no one around with finance skills then 'everyone has to chip in', which is short for 'no one wants to do it, so no one gives it proper attention', and unsurprisingly, cracks start to appear everywhere.
- **Multiple sources of truth**: You've got the information in your accounting system, the filings at Companies House and countless numbers of spreadsheets, all telling you different versions of the truth and no one pulling it all together into something simple and meaningful.
- **Over-trusting**: You are probably not trained in finance so you need to trust in the people that seemingly are. But are they as skilled as you need them to be and are they helping you to understand the information they are providing? I think there are too many amateurs in finance roles and they are wreaking havoc in small businesses in particular.

All of this leads to a lack of financial rigour and reliable reporting, without which business becomes stressful and dangerous.

When you have good financial management, knowing what decisions to make and actions to take becomes easy. The information stares you in the face and waves a big flag saying, 'this is what you need to focus on'. You can then progress with confidence and without second guessing yourself as to whether or not you are working on the right things.

It's not just about what we call financial statements, which includes the Profit & Loss (P&L) Report and Balance Sheets. It's about shining a light on the right areas and unpicking the areas that benefit from further scrutiny. Imagine knowing exactly where the opportunities and risks lie in your business and being able to ignore everything else. That's financial maturity and you are about to discover exactly how to achieve it.

Towards maturity

Clearly, financial management on its own does not equate to a successful business. Business is a multi-faceted and complex game that throws new challenges every day. That is part of the reason many of us love it so much – we enjoy problem solving.

But if the foundations are not in place, problems become storms and storms are uncontrollable. Finance is the core aspect of these foundations because, fundamentally, a business needs to make money.

Financial maturity versus financial performance

One of the reasons you set up a business was probably to make some money. I also suspect that you feel quite passionate about the field your business operates in. You need your business to achieve a certain level of financial performance in both cases for two reasons:

1. In order to provide a financial return for you and your family.
2. The business needs to work financially in order to continue your journey in your area of passion.

Without making money, you won't be able to attract and serve the dream customers for long, you won't attract and keep the best staff, and you won't give value to the world. Instead, you will be living in a world of fear, uncertainty and stress. With the right financial management in place, you will have clear visibility of the road ahead and controls to keep you on track.

Most business owners are therefore naturally seeking ideas to improve financial performance. Less are actively seeking to improve financial maturity. The reason that financial maturity is so essential, however, is because it is the precursor to financial performance. A business can't reach and maintain sustainable levels of financial performance without first having maturity. That maturity needs to exist in the people leading the company and transcend through the company itself.

When that happens and the right things are done well for a prolonged period of time, the business builds a strong platform to perform. When your agency is financially mature, it is still no guarantee of success, but your chances are far greater.

Financial maturity has many facets, which we are about to explore, but at its core it is about understanding what you want and how you are going to get it. The one thing that will always be unique about your business is that it is the only one that is built to serve you!

So, the biggest step to financial maturity is working out what you want this business to be. How much of your life do you want to give to it? What sacrifices are you willing to make and what is a step too far? There is a balance between following something that you are passionate about and losing precious time to enjoy the other aspects of your life.

Owning a business can be really exciting and rewarding. But at the same time, life can't all be about business. There are hobbies to enjoy, places to see, family and friends to spend quality time with, and of course, your precious health and fitness.

Part 2
The finance maturity curve

An agency's growth often outpaces the effectiveness of its finance function.

A well-optimized back office is essential in ensuring you are growing in the right way, but it's harder to progress further without clarity of direction and experienced financial leadership.

I set up MAP in 2013 to provide an outsourced finance function to digital agencies. Cloud accounting was taking off at the time and it gave us the ability to access our clients' real time finances quickly.

Through our experience and knowledge, we developed the financial maturity curve containing three parts: essential, enhanced and extended, in order to help our clients apply best practice.

Part 2: The finance maturity curve

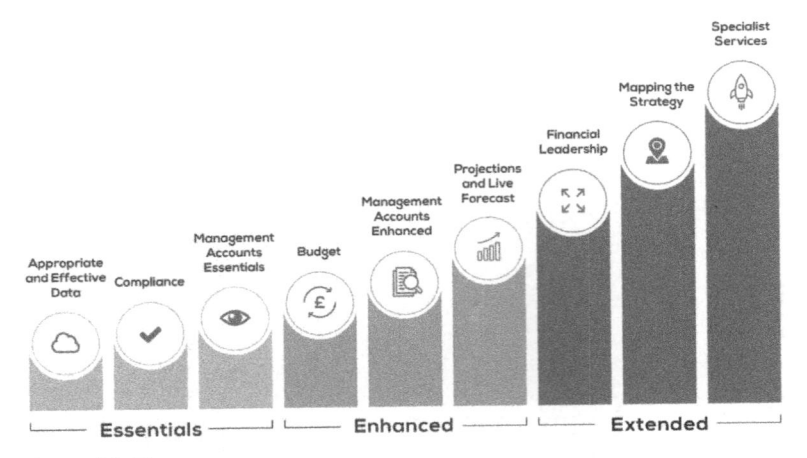

Source: MAP

The finance maturity curve is a way in which digital agencies can assess the strength of their operating model, by pegging the strengths and weaknesses of their finance function against a set of disciplines with clearly defined outcomes.

The more established the business, the further along the finance maturity curve we would expect them to be, but this may not actually be the case. Identifying areas for development shows where improvements can have the greatest impact and how long it might take to get there.

The three distinct phases of the finance maturity curve – essential, enhanced and extended – are further broken down into key elements that have proved vital for agency maturity in the following chapters. I tell you more about the MAP way in Appendix 1.

ESSENTIALS

Chapter 3
Essentials: First steps in digital agency growth

When we talk about maturity, we are referring to how well the systems and processes of the agency have developed. It's about having consistency. The right activities being carried out at the right time, by the right people and in the right way. The more mature the agency, the better it understands its data and the more integrated this data is into the business at large.

Stuart Brown, Chairman at MAP

WITHOUT THE FUNDAMENTALS installed and working well, the data relied upon for compliance and business reporting will be inaccurate and unreliable. The result makes insights blunt and decision making harder.

The purpose of 'essentials' is to understand to what extent finance is 'telling' you what is happening within your agency. This includes robust processes, as automated and real time as possible, with reporting insights delivered quickly after each month end.

☁ Appropriate and effective data: The foundation for scalable financial processes

The collection and handling of finance data has a significant impact on bottom line profitability and cash.

Leaning on the most appropriate technology is therefore essential to keep manual processing to an absolute minimum. This will also underpin the financial processes (who/what/when/how), which are the levers for understanding and controlling the flow of cash in and out.

The better the quality of data in terms of collecting and coding it correctly, the better the reporting will be down the line. The better the processes, the more you can scale capability without the need to keep adding headcount into your finance team.

As the old saying goes: 'rubbish in–rubbish out'. This has never been truer than with financial data. With all the technology now available to you to run great looking reports at the click of a button, it can be dangerous to think that accounting has become automated.

Although significant strides continue to be made in automation in financial data processing, the processes still need a guardian. That guardian will ensure that the data being processed at a transactional level is done so in line with the reporting structure of the business, asking questions like:

- Which expenditure is a cost of sale and which is an overhead?
- Which category within cost of sale or overhead does this expenditure belong to, for example, marketing or travel?
- Can we recover VAT on this expenditure?

- If there is no receipt or purchase invoice to match this bank payment against, how can we be sure what it relates to (and therefore which category to post it to)?

This might all sound like simple stuff but often it's the simple things that get neglected and when the core data is neglected, the rest of the finance function falls like a pack of cards.

Your bookkeeping systems should be integrated into the wider business processes so that those responsible for this role understand the activities of the business. The chances of recording data right at source are much greater if they truly understand three elements:

1. What the business does and how it does it.
2. The business plan and what it's trying to achieve.
3. How financial information will be presented and interpreted.

That means the bookkeeping becomes more efficient (less changes and asking questions) and gets turned around faster. Overall that leads to higher quality and more up-to-date financial information to assess and act upon. With the right processes in place to collect and process the core transactional data, the business has a platform to run meaningful reports and execute other financial tasks.

Credit control

However profitable an agency becomes, profit does not equal cash. The main driver of cash is the collection of payments from customers.

Again, automation can help massively in chasing up customers with email reminders as invoices become due for payment. This will only work if the core bookkeeping is up to date, otherwise you run the risk of customers being chased for payments that they have already made if the invoices have not been marked as paid through in your accounting system.

Otherwise, carefully crafted auto email reminders can be hugely effective. Once that system is in place, you need someone to be responsible for the traditional side of picking up the phone and having the right conversations with your customers about their payments before and after they become due.

Supplier payments

With cloud accounting technology so accessible there really is no good reason to be paying a supplier invoice from anywhere other than from within your accounting system. Paying invoices based on lists in spreadsheets, emails festering in the inbox or (perish the thought) printouts on your desk, is a thing of the past.

You want to work with one source of truth for knowing which supplier invoices are outstanding. The integrated bookkeeping system above will ensure that all of the purchase invoices that are due are easily visible in one place, digitally.

With cloud accounting applications like Xero, you can pay those invoices without leaving their platform. Moreover, by having these invoices posted in your single source of truth, you are also aiding the accuracy of financial reporting by being able to see the relevant invoices cost in the P&L or Balance Sheet reports.

Cost reviews

If you don't control your overheads, they will control you.

With the growing use of cloud technology platforms, it has never been more important to have a process for reviewing a business' overheads. We do this for a number of agencies and it is inevitable that we will find costs leaking out unnecessarily somewhere. It could be that a subscription is being paid for that is no longer in use, or it is being used but not by all of the users that you are paying for. With payment cards flying around your team and them having the ability to set up payments with usually very little authority, the risk of wastage is significant.

Again, if your data is properly maintained in your cloud accounting system, it is easy to run reports to check your regular outgoings and click in to read the detail to assess what value you are getting for the cost.

✓ Compliance: Protecting your reputation through quality and timely delivery

There are real benefits in getting your statutory requirements not just done but completed ahead of time, more accurately and stress free. Working close to the wire can put you at risk of missing deadlines – creating unwanted pressure and increasing the chance of errors.

Compliance has an important role in presenting your company to the wider world. Aspects of your reporting will be used to assess creditworthiness, and VAT or Payroll errors can bring unwanted scrutiny from HMRC. Ensuring you have a reliable and consistent way of handling compliance shouldn't just be a hygiene factor, but a signifier of a more mature approach.

If you have ambitions to sell your business one day, any buyer is going to want to see the historical information filed with Companies House, HMRC, Pension Regulators and other governing bodies. A small decision to miss a deadline or file something with errors might not affect you greatly now but it might come back to bite you when someone else is digging into your business later. Many business deals come grinding to a halt and occasionally even get aborted due to holes in its governance and reporting.

Moreover, anything filed with Companies House is visible to the public. Customers (current and prospective), suppliers, investors, lenders and potential buyers of your company will all look at your Companies House filings and draw conclusions on both the financial health of your business and its governance.

Obviously when it comes to payroll and auto enrolment pension processes, you have the added responsibility and scrutiny of your employees who will be quick to express stress and frustration if their pay is not accurate. You want these processes to be streamlined and stress free. They shouldn't involve much, if any, of your time and energy to get right.

Getting it right is the first step. Beyond that you want to offer employment packages that attract and retain the best people. In addition to a fair salary grading structure, you also have the opportunity to look at benefits that make your employees and their families feel good about you as an employer and often they will be more tax effective than a pay rise.

The government has put minimum requirement levels in place for employer pension contributions into auto enrolment schemes. Wherever your team members work now and in the future, they will get this benefit if they decide to opt in (they have to contribute themselves too if they do) so they no longer see it as a perk of working for your company. However, you have the option to pay more than the statutory minimum, which is more tax effective than a pay rise and helps your team members to save and earn compound growth until their retirement.

Bonus schemes can also be a consideration, especially in promoting and rewarding high performance. My number one rule for bonus schemes is to make sure they have a profit driver built into them. The last thing you want is to be paying bonuses out despite a lack of profit, but I've seen it happen because the scheme has been set up to be purely focused on the individual performance of the team member and no regard to how the business has performed overall.

The bonus calculator tool in Appendix 2 will help you to build a scheme that rewards individual and business performance together so that the business is never out of pocket. Essentially if you (the team) help the business to achieve more than what we are aiming for then you can share some of that excess.

Key dates

There are actually only a few key dates that all businesses need to be aware of when it comes to statutory compliance and they are listed below:

1. **VAT**: Usually quarterly
   You can apply to join the VAT Annual Accounting Scheme, which means you only file one VAT return per year, but you have to make monthly payments in advance and are left with a balancing under/over payment at the end. Quarterly is much cleaner.

   Your business' VAT quarter is not linked to the financial year end. It will be either January, February or March and then quarterly thereafter. You are required to submit each return within one month and seven days of the quarter end date. You are also required to pay the VAT due by that same date. However, if you set up a direct debit, payment will be taken three working days later, meaning there is a cash flow advantage as well as the advantage of not having to remember to manually make the payment.

2. **PAYE**: Usually monthly
   Most digital agencies will pay their salaries monthly. Any PAYE due on the salaries needs to be paid by the 22nd of the following month (or 19th if paying by post).

3. **Auto enrolment pension contributions**: Usually monthly
   Auto enrolment pension contributions due from both employer and employee are calculated as part of the payroll process. There are minimum levels that need to be met, but

both employer and employee can choose to make additional voluntary contributions if they wish.

Similar to PAYE, your business is required to submit the information of what contributions are due for each opted-in employee by the 22nd of the following month (or 19th if paying by post). This information is submitted via an upload to your company's chosen pension scheme provider.

4. **Statutory year-end accounts**: Usually annually
If your business is incorporated with Companies House (e.g. Limited Company or Limited Liability Partnership), you are required to prepare and submit financial statements annually. These reports will be publicly available, meaning anyone can view and download them.

Small companies are permitted to restrict the information that they submit. Essentially, they can exclude the profit and loss account and directors' report, which means the revenue and profit are omitted, as well as the directors' earnings and other sensitive information that you may wish to keep private. Under current rules, a company will be 'small' if it has any TWO of the following (Appendix 3:5):

- A turnover of £10.2 million or less
- £5.1 million or less on its Balance Sheet
- 50 employees or less

A company year-end date is usually the last day of a calendar month. By default, the year-end date will be the end of the month in which it incorporated. For example, a company incorporated on 18th June would have a 30th June year end. You may choose to change the year end, which may shorten or lengthen the financial period initially, before reverting back to 12-month periods thereafter.

The normal filing deadline is nine months from the year-end date, but in the first year this is earlier: one year + nine months from the date of incorporation.

5. **Corporation tax**: Usually annually
   Corporation tax is calculated based on the taxable profits of the financial period that you file the statutory accounts for. For this reason, the corporation tax return is usually prepared alongside the financial statements that get submitted to Companies House. The corporation tax return is submitted to HMRC only, along with the detailed financial statements. You cannot omit the P&L account in this case because HMRC wants to see evidence of how the corporation tax has been calculated. However, this information is private to HMRC and not publicly available, unlike Companies House submissions.

   The deadline for submitting corporation tax returns is 12 months from the year-end date. However, the deadline for paying any corporation tax due is nine months + one day following the year-end date, so the corporation tax return will still need to be prepared alongside the statutory accounts within nine months of the year end in order to calculate the corporation tax due.

6. **Confirmation statement**: Usually annually
   The second standard filing requirement with Companies House is the confirmation statement. This is an annual report of the up-to-date basic company information: registered office address, officers, business description, share capital and shareholders.

7. **Self-assessment**: Usually annually
   The requirement to complete a UK tax return depends on your circumstances.

   You must send a tax return if, in the last tax year (6th April to 5th April), any of the following applied:
   - You were self-employed as a 'sole trader' and earned more than £1,000 (before taking off anything you can claim tax relief on).
   - You were a partner in a business partnership.

- You had a total taxable income of more than £100,000.
- You had to pay capital gains tax when you sold or 'disposed of' something that increased in value.
- You had to pay the high income child benefit charge.

You may also need to send a tax return if you have any untaxed income, such as:
- Some COVID-19 grant or support payments
- Money from renting out a property
- Tips and commission
- Income from savings, investments and dividends
- Foreign income

For stakeholders in a limited company, the most likely drivers for needing a tax return are shareholders that are receiving dividends and directors earning more than £100,000 annually. The contents of your tax return will depend on your individual circumstances in terms of income sources and tax reliefs applicable.

The tax year runs from 6th April to 5th April and the filing deadline is the following 31st January. Payment for the resulting tax liability must also be settled by the filing deadline.

Payments become more complicated when the tax liability exceeds £1,000 as HMRC then requires you to make payments on account in the preceding January and July.

Here's an example of how self-assessment payments on account work:

Self-Assessment can become confusing, especially when you have a company year end that differs from the personal tax year. You need to report dividends paid in the company financial year through the statutory year-end accounts as well as dividends received in the personal tax year (6th April to 5th April) through self-assessment. If you have other sources of income it becomes more complex too, but there is no reason to leave it late and create unnecessary uncertainty and stress.

> Let's assume that your first year of requiring a self-assessment return is 2024/25 and your tax liabilities became as follows:
>
> Tax liability for 2024/25:   £800
>
> Tax liability for 2025/26:   £2,000
>
> Tax liability for 2026/27:   £3,000
>
> Payment due 31st January 2026:
> £800 liability
>
> Payment due 31st January 2027:
> £2,000 liability + (50% × £2,000 POA 1) = £3,000
>
> Payment due 31st July 2027:
> (50% × £2,000) = £1,000 POA 2
>
> Payment due 31st January 2028:
> £3,000 liability − £1,000 POA 1 − £1,000 POA 2 = £1,000 balancing payment + (50% × £1,500 POA 1) = £1,750
>
> *POA = Payment*

You can get ahead by running calculations during and shortly after the tax year, without waiting for the formal production of your tax return. In Appendix 2 you will find a personal tax forecasting tool that allows you to quickly calculate the tax liability resulting from your sources and levels of income. You can use this throughout the year to look at hypothetical scenarios so it can also serve as a decision-making tool if you are considering different levels of income and investments.

Insolvency

There is no taboo in admitting financial distress or admitting an insolvency. Often it is the fear of failure that stops entrepreneurs from seeking help, and most of the time when an entrepreneur does decide to reach out for experts' assistance, it is at a very late stage.

The earlier someone seeks advice the better, as the problem can be more easily solved and there will be more options available to the company to overcome the issue(s).

I wanted to cover the subject of insolvency in this book for two reasons:

1. Too often business owners hide from the subject, which makes it so much worse than it needs to be. The more aware you are of the vital signs, your responsibilities and your options, the better equipped you are to act quickly and reduce the problem instead of escalating it.
2. More businesses go through periods of distress than you might imagine. Some of the most successful businesses in the world have been close to the edge, but they recovered because they acted quickly and took the right advice.

Jimmy Fish is a Licenced Insolvency Practitioner and I asked him for his guidance to business owners who find their businesses in financial distress. Here's what he said.

Interview with Jimmy Fish, Licenced Insolvency Practitioner

What is an Insolvency Practitioner?

An Insolvency Practitioner (IP) is an Officer of the Court who is licensed by an authorized regulatory body to undertake formal insolvency appointments within the UK.

Only licenced IPs are authorized to act on behalf of companies, and individuals, when they are facing insolvency or financial distress. An IP's decisions about what to do with an insolvent company or individual will be based on what process results in the best return for creditors.

In its simplest form, an IP realizes assets and distributes the proceeds to creditors. IPs are licensed and regulated, and their fees are agreed with creditors or the courts.

Transparency is at the heart of any process and the IP's fees and reports about their cases are filed with Companies House and are publicly available.

What is the legal definition of insolvency?

A company is insolvent if it has insufficient assets to discharge its debts and liabilities.

There are different tests to determine insolvency, depending on the context in which the expression is used.

Section 123 of the Insolvency Act 1986 defines the tests of insolvency as:

Balance sheet test = liabilities outweigh assets

Cash flow test = cannot pay debts as and when due

What are the responsibilities of the company director in this matter?

Directors are responsible for the day-to-day management of their companies. Their role is set out in company law, the company's constitution (Articles of Association) and, if they have employees, their employment contracts.

Directors owe legal duties, such as the duty to promote the success of the company for the benefit of its shareholders. But when a company is in financial difficulty and there is a risk of insolvency, directors owe a primary duty of care to creditors to minimize their losses.

What are the three most common errors/issues that lead to insolvency?

The mix of poor financial management and a consistent lack of appropriate cash levels is one of the biggest causes of insolvency. Most small business owners are good at their craft, as a designer or a web engineer, for example, but they are not accountants and can find it difficult to stay on top of the books and figures, which results in a lack of reliable, up-to-date, financial information.

Budgeting plays a big part in effective financial management in that a solid budget can often predict the highs and lows of the business cycle and so allow you to make better decisions in areas such as spending and cash collection. Also in the smaller business, we often see the owner/

directors failing to separate business and personal accounts, running personal expenses through the business.

If your business is laden with too much debt, then this is always a challenge. The same is true if you don't have an effective debt recovery procedure in place to make sure you get your money when it is owed.

But the biggest mistake we see is not taking advice sooner and battling on too long. Burying your head in the sand only further increases the chances of insolvency and facing any financial hardship head on may open up your options and help you steady the ship before it's too late!

Where do you see companies continue to trade insolvently, not knowing or understanding?

One area that is often entered into with the best of intentions, is where the proverbial carrot gets dangled on a new contract and the business rushes to increase resources at their own cost.

Complex projects also must have a clear and understood payment schedule within them, so the supplier is not holding all that cost without payment until the last possible moment.

It is also important to remember that we simply don't know what we don't know and all too often it is hard for the directors to recognize the signs, or worse have denial, where we see directors pumping personal money into companies to stop them having to make what are difficult decisions.

What are the process options?

There are typically four options for companies unable to pay their debts as they fall due:

1. **Company voluntary arrangement (CVA)**

    This is a formal agreement with creditors to repay debt over time. This may be at a discount, or sometimes written off, depending on the agreement of all the secured and preferential creditors plus at least 75% of unsecured creditors.

    One of the attractions of a CVA is that the company remains as a going concern.

2. **Administration**

    We can see a good business with contracts and employees to preserve, but too much debt and creditor pressure is making life difficult, if not impossible. Here the IP files for a period of moratorium to relieve creditor pressure while the business and assets are marketed for sale, once an independent valuation of the business and assets is made.

The best bits are sold to a new limited company and the creditors are left behind with the old company, where the creditors seek to share any cash realizations after costs. Under this process employees will often transfer with the business under TUPE (Transfer of Undertakings (Protection of Employment)) regulations, and so administration can be the preferred route for employees.

The business is sold to the highest bidder, which may be a competitor, but can also be the old directors, known as a connected party, subject to a high level of scrutiny and reporting requirements.

3. **Creditors' voluntary liquidation (CVL)**

   CVL is where directors voluntarily decide to close their business down because it has become insolvent and therefore cannot legally continue trading. Often as the result of a terminal insolvency event, such as the loss of a major contract or client.

   The business ceases to trade as it is no longer viable, and the company has effectively come to the end of its economic life. Liquidation results in the formal winding up of the company and the redundancies of all staff who can claim against the government's redundancy payments services. There is no salvaging of the business and any assets are sold at auction.

   The directors can purchase the assets at fair value and can set up again post liquidation but will be automatically prohibited from using a name similar to that of the previous company that is in liquidation. Again, an independent valuation of the assets is key to this strategy.

4. **Compulsory liquidation**

   The process that is out of the hands of the company is when the company is wound up by the Court, resulting in investigations by the Insolvency Service.

What does life look like for the directors involved following insolvency?

Putting aside the significant disappointment and maybe embarrassment associated with insolvency, there is not as much effect as many believe.

If you wish to continue in the same line as the old business, then you may struggle getting credit from a supplier, sometimes having to pay higher prices or pay on a pro-forma basis.

Existing contracts may also be at risk, as there is often an insolvency clause of a supply contract that allows the buyer to cancel any agreement.

On a personal level for the director of a limited company there is limited liability, where the debts fall away with the company unless any personal guarantees exist. And a company failure has no impact on personal status, such as credit ratings, as the public record is against the company and not against their name.

Where personal liability can occur is when the IP is obliged to investigate the conduct of directors and identifies any areas of misconduct that could result in claims to be pursued for the benefit of all creditors.

Here the IP has a number of powers available to them to track down missing assets, reverse pre-insolvency transactions and investigate wrongdoing by individuals and company directors.

What leads to a director's ban?

Director disqualification proceedings can be launched if it is believed that a director has been involved in (or has allowed others to be involved in) unfit conduct.

'Unfit conduct' includes:

- Allowing a company to continue trading when it can't pay its debts.
- Not keeping proper company accounting records.
- Not sending accounts and returns to Companies House.
- Not paying tax owed by the company.
- Using company money or assets for personal benefit.
- Taking deposits for services they knew wouldn't be supplied/worsening the position of creditor(s).

Serious misconduct occurs where a loss to creditors exists due to theft, preference payments, transactions at an undervalue, wrongful trading or excessive remuneration. This can lead to a criminal investigation.

Section 212 of the Insolvency Act 1986 addresses the legal concept of misfeasance and makes a director personally accountable to pay back to the company the amount of the loss caused by any misfeasance to the extent that the Court so orders.

I certainly hope that this situation does not come into your business, but it is important to understand how to recognize the signs early and then how you can reach out for help and support.

Many issues I see are simply down to ignorance... but ignorance is not a defence!

Jimmy Fish, Licenced Insolvency Practitioner

I hope that insolvency is not something that your business ever experiences but that's not to say it's shameful if it does. This guidance should help you to navigate the situation effectively and come back fighting on the other side.

◎ Management accounts: Essentials: An accurate account of financial activity

Effective conversations around business performance begin when the intelligence is there and shared for all to see. At the essential level, this is about assessing trends based on sound historical fact.

Meaningful P&L and Balance Sheet reporting are at the core, and the more that these can be reliably compared to prior periods, the more information is released back to the management team. Once you know what you are looking at today, you can move forward more confidently tomorrow.

Revenue recognition and the accruals concept

One of the most fundamental aspects of financial reporting for agencies is the accruals concept.

On the face of it I can understand how it sounds like accounting jargon, but it's actually a very simple concept that you really need to understand. Essentially, when you run financial reports from your accounting system ahead of a month end routine, the information is going to be incomplete (and therefore misleading) for this reason: *it is only a reflection of sales invoices raised, purchase invoices received and bank transactions reconciled.*

If you raised a sales invoice to the value of £120,000 in the month, you will see £120,000 of revenue in the P&L. If that invoice was in fact for 12 months of services billed in advance, only one month's worth of revenue (1/12 × £120k) has been earned in the first month.

'Earned' is not a reference to cash. Ignore cash at this stage. Earned refers to the value of the work that has actually been delivered. If you're only 1/12th of the way through the work, you have only earned 1/12th of the value.

To complete this picture, the costs that you have incurred against this revenue also belong in the same month as the earned revenue. If you have had salaried team members, freelancers, or other third party costs associated with the revenue from this client, you need to see these costs in the same period as the earned revenue in order to make meaningful observations.

Let's illustrate the difference between a P&L and Balance Sheet before and after applying the accruals concept.

Imagine the costs associated with the £120,000 contract above are as follows:

- Salaries   £36k paid monthly
- Freelancers   £24k billed quarterly

The accruals method in action:

	Before	After
Revenue	£120,000	£10,000
Salaries	£3,000	£3,000
Freelancers	—	£2,000
Profit	£115,000	£5,000

A drastic profit difference of £110,000!

You can see that the real profit on this contract in the first month is £5,000 because your resources cost one month of salary at £3,000 plus one month of freelancer cost at £2,000, and you have delivered 1/12th of the £120,000 contract = £10,000 in revenue.

Before these adjustments, you had a £120,000 sales invoice distorting the revenue and the freelancer bill won't land in your accounting system until the end of the quarter, so that cost is missing.

Finance's job at month end is to *defer* £110,000 of the £120,000 revenue and *accrue* £2k of freelancer costs. The invoices are unchanged. You bill that £120,000 as quickly as you can and get paid as soon as you can too! The fact that freelancers are billing quarterly in arrears is also great for cash flow.

But accounting (and meaningful financial reporting) isn't driven by invoice dates or cash being paid, it's based on when revenue is earned and costs are incurred. That's the accruals concept.

A wakeup call for a failing digital agency

We once started working with an agency that thought they had a healthy business. It didn't take long to identify that they were running their financial reports without a month end exercise to apply the accruals concept and it had a massive impact. They were billing large sums for projects in advance, so the profitability looked amazing!

This misleading information was causing them to over trade. They were hiring like crazy and investing substantially in sales and marketing to accelerate more growth. When we adjusted their accounts to show the true financial performance, it was a far cry from the picture they had been seeing in their previous financial reports. The profitability was nothing like what they had seen because they had only earned a fraction of the revenue that they had previously reported.

Imagine the isolated example presented above, but for all of their projects! It was a huge wake up call for their business to find that they were in fact losing money on their work, so they were growing something that was loss making and the problem was getting bigger and bigger.

The knock on effects of this were huge:

- They kept hiring more staff even though it was clear that each staff member was losing, not making, them money.
- They kept taking on new clients, again who were costing the business more than the revenue generated.
- They took their eye off basic credit control since they assumed cash wouldn't be a problem with such a 'profitable' business.
- They didn't pay attention to profitability at a client or project level; again, because seemingly they were the most profitable agency ever!
- The sales and growth culture led to huge over servicing issues as they lacked control over making projects run on time and charging for extra work orders.

Ultimately, the accruals concept has to be applied in order to understand profitability. Without it, your financial reports are just a reflection of what you have billed and who has billed you, which is of very little use. This approach doesn't even provide a cash flow outlook, since it's based on billed dates and not the case due dates.

The other side of the accruals concept equation

Another fundamental aspect of accounting is the double entry system. Quite simply this dictates that for every accounting entry there must be an equal matching entry – or for every debit there must be a credit.

In the earlier example, £110,000 of revenue was deferred but where does it go? That £110,000 that has been deducted from the revenue in the P&L is added as a liability in the Balance Sheet. Practically, the business has billed for something that it hasn't yet earned and so the client is probably within their rights to ask for a credit against that invoice if your agency can no longer deliver the contracted work. The first £10,000 wouldn't get credited because that work has been done and the revenue is therefore earned. But for the other £110,000 that becomes a liability until it is earned.

Each month the £110,000 is reduced by £10,000, which is then moved to revenue in the P&L. By the end of the 12 months, the agency has earned the full £120,000 in the P&L and the liability is down to nil in the Balance Sheet.

No one expects you to be able to see into the future, but you can manage the near term effectively with the right elements in place. Having this sense of being able to understand what might happen in the future – even if you are unable to predict it – provides clarity and can reduce stressful situations into something that can be looked at rationally.

Will Jarvis, Head of Financial Controls at MAP

With core financial processes in place, you have the assurance of having a sound understanding to help you in the future, whatever develops. Figure 3.1. demonstrates the core financial processes in place.

Figure 3.1. Core financial processes in place

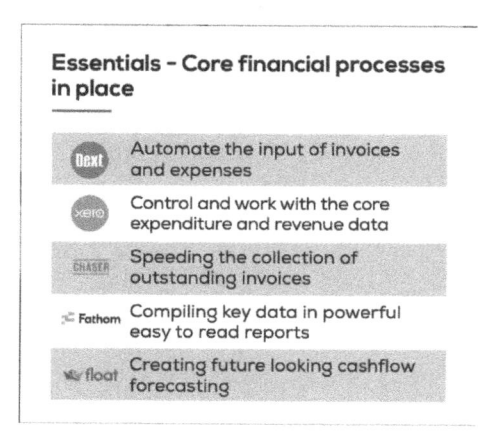

Essentials – Core financial processes in place

- **Dext** — Automate the input of invoices and expenses
- **xero** — Control and work with the core expenditure and revenue data
- **Chaser** — Speeding the collection of outstanding invoices
- **Fathom** — Compiling key data in powerful easy to read reports
- **float** — Creating future looking cashflow forecasting

Source: MAP

ENHANCED

Chapter 4
Enhanced: From numbers to narrative

A FOCUS ON the enhanced aspects of your finance function allows you to align your business much closer to your overall objectives and to create a powerful narrative around progress.

Having this sense of being able to understand what is happening now, and what might happen in the future, is an important signal to financial maturity, as is welcoming in the voice of an independent finance partner.

ⓔ Budget

A detailed and achievable plan for the next 12 months

Agencies can claim to have a budget in place, but it is important to have confidence that it has been produced following a thorough and meaningful process. A 12-month budget needs to be modelled around key areas and reporting requirements, and not just a narrow view of sales or core costs.

A good budget will include an accompanying capacity plan, marketing plan, Balance Sheet and cash flow. It should consider departmental reporting and recognition of different types of revenue. An effective budget therefore is a key part of your business plan for the year ahead.

This is your business, it's your plan, and you are in control of delivering it.

The first step of the process is to understand from you as the business owner what the bigger picture objectives are and what that means for you personally. Amongst all the noise of running a business day to day, this is the annual opportunity to take a step back, challenge the reasons why the business exists and understand if you are on the right track.

If the business is going into a new financial year in a strong position, in good market conditions, the revenue targets that you set in the budget should push you to make the most of the good times. One agency we worked with had been steadily growing but suggested that, as much as they would love to, they could never see the business achieving a £200,000 revenue month. They were an established business, having been trading for over a decade, and this became a glass ceiling that they had been trying to break through for years but had never quite been able to achieve.

We built a revenue forecast to grow from where they were currently, but that was grounded in data. We worked out the contracted revenue that already existed from current clients, and then worked through live opportunities for both existing and prospective clients. Then we were able to calculate the balance needed to reach the £200,000 month and the target total financial year revenue. We then started to look at the number of leads that would need to be generated based on their typical sales conversion rate and put a sales and marketing plan together to give confidence that it could be achieved.

After more than ten years of trying, they hit their £200,000 number within the next 12 months. To think a spreadsheet of target figures was what drove this achievement would be naive. It was the change in culture that this planning process started that made the difference. The directors had confidence that the number was in reach and that they had a plan to get them there. I can't emphasize enough how important this change in belief is for a business. People typically see a business plan as a report – something tangible that sits on their desk or up on the wall. That is the output but it's the process that drives the momentum in the business.

When we're taken through a process that requires an investment in time and energy, it means a lot more than being handed a piece of paper that someone else has produced. You get the opportunity to discuss, debate, sharpen your thinking and ultimately gain clarity on what it is you want and how you are going to get it. It should be an uplifting exercise that begins a chain of events that sparks energy and confidence through your business.

When you invest this time, you are far more likely to stay focused on the execution. If the process was quick and easy, there is a danger that it won't win your heart and mind. The plan will get forgotten just as quickly as was formed.

To be clear, I am not suggesting you make the budgeting and planning process complicated. I recommend that you use a tool that enables you to seamlessly pull the information together. If you follow a framework for how to go about this process, it means you put less energy into what the steps need to be and more focus on doing the work.

You will find a tool for working through and compiling the budget in Appendix 2. I hope you find the process as enlightening and helpful as our clients do. There is nothing like having a plan that is meaningful to you and that you believe you will achieve.

Initial time should then be spent analyzing the prior years and the trajectory in which the revenue, costs and profit have changed. There will be learnings to take away, both good and bad, which will factor into the budget being built for the next 12 months.

A base budget can be built based on the 'as-is' position so that before anything else we can see the total cost base and the break-even point. From there you can make adjustments and run different scenarios. It may be that you want to make four new hires in the year or invest in a particular marketing campaign that involves a higher spend than usual. You can see the impact those decisions will have on both profit and cash flow.

From the cost analysis exercise, you will have an initial view of what the required revenue is to cover break-even and then to deliver a certain level of profit. The reliance on external costs and freelancers will need to be considered at this stage and from that the anticipated gross profit margin.

When it comes to the profit figure being targeted, it is important not to fall into the trap of building a budget based on 'last year plus a bit more'. Ultimately, the profit target should be generated from the bigger picture conversation of where you want the business to be in x number of years and what that means for your personal wealth or the business valuation. You can then work back from there.

The next step is to map out what the revenue looks like. You will have a level of confirmed work already, which becomes the starting point. Any shortfall to target can then be built up by understanding the clients you work with; if they are on retainers or projects, and what the numbers need to look like in terms of new client acquisition and average client spend. You can then give feedback on how that feels and what is achievable. At this point it is also useful to consider what the key drivers are to the financial results, and what Key Performance Indicators (KPIs) should be being tracked throughout the year.

Some further thought will now be required on any alterations required to costs. From building a capacity plan, we can see if the team you have is capable of delivering the revenue target. Based on the new business requirement it shows, it may be that the marketing budget needs some tweaking to generate enough new leads.

Ultimately, a budget should be the right level of ambition but realistic. The aim is for you to go away from the process feeling excited and clear on what you need to do to achieve the figures – but also why the targets exist and what it means for you personally. That is what gives you the purpose and the drive to deliver on it day to day.

Capacity plan

A key component of a budget is a capacity plan.

As the ultimate driver of profitability for an agency is people, we need to understand how to resource the business to achieve its revenue and profit goals. Building a capacity plan will identify issues and opportunities for the size and shape of the team, setting the stage for a strategic and sustainable business model.

Bloat versus burnout

One common challenge is understanding the delicate balance between having a team that is too large, resulting in bloat and squeezed profit margins, and a team that is too small, leading to burnout, compromised quality and potential team attrition. The first step in addressing this challenge is a comprehensive diagnosis.

Understanding the revenue model: Time for money

Regardless of the pricing strategy (time and materials, fixed fees or value pricing), your team is the biggest cost. The revenue model must cover the cost of their time, overheads and provide a margin for consistent profitability.

Building a capacity plan model: Practical steps

A capacity plan serves as a key planning tool in a service business, offering a structured approach to assessing and optimizing your team's potential for revenue generation.

In essence, a capacity plan is a dynamic tool that allows agencies to align their workforce with the demands of their workload. It goes beyond mere headcounts, providing a detailed breakdown of each team member's role, availability and potential for chargeable client work.

By crafting a robust capacity plan, agencies gain a clear understanding of their team's capacity, allowing for informed decision making, resource allocation and revenue forecasting.

Achievable revenue with a 5% increase in utilization can be seen in Figure 4.1:

Figure 4.1. Capacity plan with improved utilization

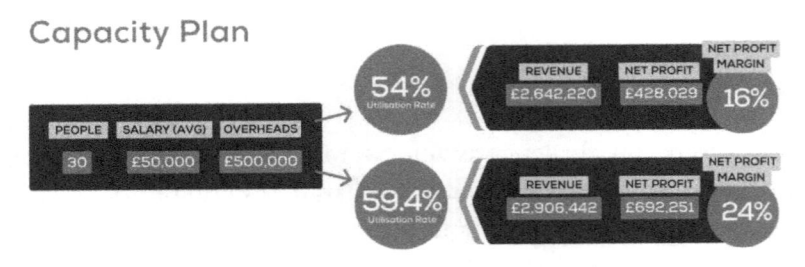

Capacity Plan

PEOPLE	SALARY (AVG)	OVERHEADS
30	£50,000	£500,000

Utilisation Rate	REVENUE	NET PROFIT	NET PROFIT MARGIN
54%	£2,642,220	£428,029	16%
59.4%	£2,906,442	£692,251	24%

Source: MAP

In this illustration, a 10% increase in utilization results in an additional £264,222 on the bottom line.

Now, let's delve into the practical steps involved in building a comprehensive capacity plan model for your digital agency:

1. **List employees by role**: Create a comprehensive list of all employees in your business, categorized by role.
2. **Enter salaries and working days**: Input employee salaries, working days per year, holidays and other time off.
3. **Assign utilization rates**: Define the proportion of time each role can be expected to spend on chargeable client work.
4. **Calculate net billable days**: Compute the net 'billable' days for each employee, considering their availability for client work.
5. **Enter day rates**: List each employee's day rate, considering blended rates or variations based on roles.

Analyzing the revenue model: Profit per employee

Once the data has been crunched, zoom out and assess the story that is being presented.

- **Compute total revenue capacity**: Calculate the total revenue capacity per month and year based on the listed team.
- **Evaluate profit per employee**: Focus on the profit per employee rather than revenue to understand the overall profitability of each role.
- **Identify opportunities and challenges**: Analyze the model to identify areas of strength, resource gaps and potential revenue generation opportunities.

Taking action: Leveraging insights

- **Addressing imbalances**: Act on insights gained from the model. Adjust team sizes in specific roles or seek additional revenue based on your team's capacity.

- **Exploring revenue streams**: Explore revenue opportunities within your existing client base and seek the right type of revenue based on your team's capabilities.
- **Consulting with experts**: Book a session with one of our team to discuss and stress-test your model.

Building a digital agency that makes sense involves a careful balance between team size and revenue generation. By leveraging a capacity plan model, you gain clarity on your team's potential, identify opportunities for growth and ensure a profitable and sustainable business model.

Don't just *run* your agency blindly – *model it* for success.

The cost of an hour

Once you know the cost of a day of each team member's time, you can obviously calculate that down to the hourly cost. Let's say the hourly cost of the average works out at £70 and you charge them out at £120.

Every hour that they work, they make £50 for the business, but for every hour that they don't work they cost the business £70! It's quite frightening when looked at like that. Imagine if you then multiply that by the number of people in your business and the number of hours they spend on non-chargeable work.

It feels horrible to view people as stock. Of course they are not, but for the purpose of making money in a service business, the same principles of eroding stock apply. Once that hour has gone, it can't be made back up. Try asking a team member to forgo their salary for the hour that didn't generate revenue…

So, as crude as it sounds, applying the principles of eroding stock to people's time helps to frame the required thinking to build a profitable agency. The solution is not to become so obsessed that suddenly everyone is expected to deliver chargeable work for every hour. If that was the case, no one would get trained, there would be no new ideas getting generated and you'd have a very tired and dissatisfied team.

The capacity plan enables you to look at this clearly and build a model that allows for the right balance of chargeable and non-chargeable activity. Enough to build a financially healthy, but sustainable, business.

Management accounts: advanced
Extending your finance pack into further areas

Having historical data in an optimized view helps to bring important trends to the attention of your decision makers. This is transformed, however, when it becomes a tool to assess performance against your budget, and particularly with an independent finance voice at the table.

While the figures describe a point in time, a finance professional can describe what is driving those numbers, what patterns are occurring in the data and why it is important. They provide opinion, insight and analysis – the narrative behind the numbers.

With your budget in place and clarity on the route map to achieving the financial goals of the business, monthly management accounts can then be used to track progress. Accounts should ideally be produced within two weeks of month end to give you as the business owner prompt insights so that any learnings can be implemented quickly.

I'm an advocate of a simplified management accounts pack that includes an overview of the financial KPIs, a P&L Report and a Balance Sheet. All too often do we start working with agencies who have an extremely detailed management accounts pack in place. While data is important, often the wood can't be seen for the trees, and it's very difficult to understand what the key takeaways are. Your accounts pack should be simple and effective. For any areas where more detail is needed then that information is always available behind the scenes and additional reports can be run.

The key function of your P&L Report is variance analysis to the budget that has been set. While the numbers and the margins can be looked at generically and benchmarked against industry standards, the best insights come from tracking against your own budget and what good looks like for your agency specifically, based on the trajectory you are on.

Each row should be considered in isolation – from revenue differences and through each of the cost differences you are seeing. If you are down on revenue or profit, challenge what can be done in the coming months to get things back on track.

While your P&L is a report of the financial performance over a given period, the Balance Sheet is a snapshot of the financial position and the assets and liabilities you have at a given date. Often it can be overlooked in favour of the P&L but it's equally as important.

Learnings should be taken on how robust the business is through key ratios such as current assets versus current liabilities, how well you're doing at generating cash and any upcoming risks there may be. The bottom line is the equity or net assets in the business – the overall result of total assets less total liabilities. If you're profitable, this figure will be gradually increasing month on month.

When it comes to agency financial reporting, I see both ends of the extreme. Some are driving blindly with little more reporting than what they are required to do by law. They have no idea of the financial performance for the latest period and they are living in hope. They track who needs to pay them and who they need to pay to 'manage cash flow' and they get stuck in the survival cycle. When an agency is run like this, it can never possibly thrive because instead of seeking opportunities to scale the business through high marking opportunities, it is focused on having enough cash to pay the bills. It is a game of 'avoiding defeat' rather than playing to win and it will inevitably end in disaster.

At the other extreme, there are agencies with so much data they don't know what to do with it. They have read all the books, watched all the webinars and listened to the gurus on stage telling them about all the things they must track if they are going to have a successful business. They are good students and do their homework, producing detailed reports full of metrics and ratios. The problem is that they have put so much energy into pulling the data together, they are now drowning in it and it becomes really difficult to make meaningful observations.

I spoke with Nikki Gatenby, a Non-Executive Director (NED) for Digital Agencies about the key metrics she advises agencies to track and here's what she had to say.

Nikki Gatenby's commercial health check

There are headline commercial KPIs and benchmarks to give you insight beyond the Profit & Loss Report and Balance Sheet. These are insightful to track because they give you an indication of the health of your agency commercials at a glance.

1. Revenue (not turnover, so taking out those client-pass-through costs).
2. Gross profit percent: Knowing what it is right now and what you're aiming for, ideally, at least 50%.
3. Net profit: Ideally, double digit. Over 15% is good.
4. Profitability by client: Can you track it? Can you see it? And can you see where the issues are?
5. Client concentration: What percentage of your revenue or your gross profit does each client represent? Is any one client worth more than your net profit? If the majority of your revenue or profit is concentrated into one or two clients, you may need to look at rebalancing this to reduce your risk of over-reliance on them.

6. Pipeline value: What's your forecasted pipeline value and weighted value? Not everything in your pipeline comes in; know the likelihood of conversion to help you plan your future revenue and resourcing.

7. Months of overhead cover: Your cash in the bank – how many months could you keep trading if no more future revenue came in as of tomorrow? Ideally, this is three plus months, six plus is way better – as a global pandemic has taught us.

8. Compensation to revenue: The level of compensation you are paying to all staff and freelancers (including the founders/directors) as a percent of your overall revenue. The ideal is between 45% and 55%. If you're running a lot higher than that, you potentially have too many people in the business, maybe have too high a salary bill, or you've not got enough business because there's too many hours not being sold. If it's way lower, you could be pricing brilliantly, or maybe you're not paying people enough, or maybe you've got too much going on which could lead to burnout. Either way a number outside of the ideal needs attention.

9. Revenue per person: This needs to be in context of your average salary. There's an industry 'rule-of-thumb' number of around £100,000 of RPP. However, if you're a consultancy, and everyone's paid £100,000+ salary, they need to generate a higher revenue per person to generate profit. So a healthy RPP is totally dependent on your average salary. The RPP you should be looking for is about 2.5x your average salary.

10. Utilization: Have you got everyone billed out to the right level? Are they utilized to the right degree? What's the potential in your team in terms of what you're not billing out? What's the economic headroom? What could you do if you were getting that revenue? What choices would that provide you with – and what freedom?

11. Non-billable/Billable team: This changes as your business grows, but 1:4 is probably the maximum; ideally, 1:6. Interesting to know those numbers and how you're tracking them going forward.

12. Employees/Freelancers: Ideally, no less than 10% freelancers in your business, This gives you flexibility as our agency resource rarely matches our workload day to day.

These commercial health check numbers enable you to understand the vitality of your agency. Talking them through with your team can generate strong positive action to increase the health of your business overall.

Nikki Gatenby, a Non-Executive Director (NED) for Digital Agencies

Nikki talked through these key metrics in our recorded webinar on 'Profit Culture'. There is a link to the recording in Appendix 2.

📈 Projections

Using data and judgement to map out likely scenarios

Projections play an important role in helping to map out the likelihood of meeting the budget and to explore scenarios that provide opportunities or help manage risk.

For truly effective projections, overheads and revenue need to be updated continuously, and integrated with a live view of target, converted and quoted revenue. Not only does this depend on the consistent quality of financial data, but also the integrity of the sales pipeline.

This is your car. You decide where you want to go; you have several routes to get you there, and you are in control of choosing which one you are going to take. But if you switch off the satnav, you might end up lost at sea. Forecasting, like having the satnav switched on, is de-risking failing to reach your destination on time.

Management accounts by nature are a backwards looking view of what has already happened in the business. With the right financial forecasts in place alongside them, nothing that is ever shared in the monthly accounts should come as a surprise.

Live financial forecasts give a view of the confirmed revenue and the expected costs of the agency for the coming months. The key word in the previous sentence is 'confirmed', as the starting point should be for the forecast to include confirmed revenue only. Due to the project nature of many agencies that will often give a difficult view of the coming months, particularly when you get three plus months out; however, that view is essential to understand the shortfalls and what action can be taken to bridge the gap.

The costs of the agency do tend to be more predictable with the biggest spend coming from your employed team and supporting freelancers. With an updated view of expected costs, the projected profit figure can be understood early in the day. The forecasted revenue, costs and profit can then be compared to your budget. If the numbers are lower, then also comparing to your break-even point can be useful so you know specifically what needs to happen as a minimum.

Once you know the shortfall of confirmed revenue against your targets, a forecast of new business requirements comes in, allowing you and the team to discuss what opportunities you have to make up any gap. As you continue to collate this data you'll start to have a better understanding of what the numbers mean and what you need to see in the pipeline to be reassured that you're on track. What varies agency to agency is the conversion rate and the conversion time, so make sure to spend time working out what applies to you.

Live forecasting is all about making effective decisions early and minimizing any surprises. Revenue forecasting works particularly well as part of a weekly routine, giving the team who can influence those numbers clarity, accountability and momentum.

With the above trio of reporting in place and the principles being stuck to, you're giving your agency the best chance of success – whatever that success looks like for you.

Why and when to forecast cash flow

My hope is that by following the principles in this book, cash flow becomes less of an issue. If your business is highly profitable and works to short credit terms with customers, it should be flush with cash. The focus therefore should be on profit and credit control.

Cash flow forecasting is therefore not always necessary. It requires a significant investment of someone's time (which the business will have to pay for) to maintain a cash flow forecast. For these reasons, I often find myself talking businesses out of maintaining a cash flow forecast. If all it's telling you is how many hundreds of thousands of pounds are going to be in the bank, it's not very useful. On the other hand, if there is a genuine risk of running out of cash, you need to be able to rely on a forecast in order to make difficult decisions, such as:

- How do we know if we can afford which suppliers to pay this week?
- Are we able to pay this upcoming tax liability?
- Do we need additional funding?
- Can we afford to engage with that contractor/hire that employee?

Ultimately, the purpose of the forecast is to predict the future cash balance at a specific period so that these questions can be asked.

A cash flow forecast is a financial tool used by businesses to project the cash inflows and cash outflows over a period and is designed to be directionally correct. A cash flow forecast typically includes:

- **Cash inflows**: These are the sources of cash, such as sales revenue, investments, loans or other sources of income.
- **Cash outflows**: These are the expenses and payments that will be made, including operating expenses, salaries, loan repayments, taxes and other expenditures.
- **Opening balance**: The amount of cash available at the beginning of the forecast period.
- **Closing balance**: The projected cash balance at the end of the forecast period, calculated by adding the cash inflows and subtracting the cash outflows from the opening balance.

By creating a cash flow forecast, businesses can anticipate periods of surplus or shortfall in cash and take proactive measures to manage their finances effectively. It helps in identifying potential cash shortages, allowing for adjustments in spending or seeking additional funding if necessary. Additionally, it aids in evaluating the financial health of a business and assessing its ability to meet financial obligations in the future.

Getting started

First, identify the sources of incoming cash and the drivers of outgoing cash. These should be documented and be as detailed as possible (subscriptions may seem immaterial but it can be eye-opening when they are all listed together). All of these sources should then be collated into a clear summary – this should contain your opening balance, net cash movement and your predicted closing balance. The period typically covered in a cash flow forecast is 13 weeks and it gives you a quarterly view.

There are many other considerations when building a cash flow forecast, if you have other financial forecasts in place these can give you a head start on pulling the data together, another key resource is bank statements as they are the source of truth.

Although the forecast is designed to be directionally correct, where you have got the information to be detailed try and include this where possible to minimize the risk of the forecast showing you a false projection.

Now with the build complete, the most important part is understanding it and keeping your eye on it.

Keeping your eyes on the cash flow

The best routine for reviewing the forecast is weekly or fortnightly and should be concurrent with credit control updates and supplier payment runs. The credit control update should provide visibility of the immediate cash coming into the business, which should then help you decide which suppliers should be prioritized before making blind payment runs.

As with any forecast, reality can differ. Maybe a customer hasn't paid on time or a purchase invoice has been missing and requires payment immediately; this is why it is important to stick to a routine to review and understand what has driven those differences. This data will then help prioritize what to do with the cash available and this is also the point where you will quickly identify what is causing the cash strain and you can start to consider implementing changes.

Experiencing a cash strain can be incredibly stressful, not only do you have the pressure of delivering for your business but now with an added worry of whether you have the funds to support it. Some of the suggestions below may help consider which areas of your agency you can review to help your cash position:

1. **Cash inflows**
    - Efficient invoicing process, ensuring invoices are raised and sent as soon as possible.
    - Consider alternate sources of revenue.
    - Can we take deposits?
    - Can we invoice earlier on in the project?
    - Are all recurring invoices automatically sent out?
    - Do we have direct debits set up, where possible?
    - Ensuring all recharged costs are tracked and recharged in full (unless the agreement states otherwise).
    - Strict payment terms agreed with customers.

2. **Cash outflows**
    - Take advantage of payment terms offered by suppliers.
    - Negotiate payment plans where possible.
    - Prioritize supplier payments that have the biggest impact on the operations of the business (does this directly generate cash?).

- Regularly question if your expenses are necessary.

These suggestions should be regularly reviewed even once you've stabilized your cash flow situation to build resilience and avoid similar challenges in the future.

While it might not be rocket science, cash flow forecasting does require a lot of management and diligence to make it credible. You need someone to be all-in on managing it effectively because when cash is that tight, you need information that you can rely upon being accurate.

If cash is tight in your business right now, download the free cash flow forecasting tool in Appendix 2.

How much cash should I have in my business?

When running a business, you need to make sure that you are retaining at least enough cash for working capital. Ideally, you should have additional cash reserves available to fund one-off expenditure or a downturn in trade.

So how much cash should you have at any given moment?

Crunching the numbers

Working capital is often a mis-understood concept because it gets calculated and explained in different ways. Essentially, it is the amount of cash that can easily be accessed after accounting for all short-term liabilities being set aside.

In technical terms, it is current assets minus current liabilities.

Relevant current assets in a digital agency are most likely to be:

- Cash
- Receivables/trade debtors (money owed by customers)
- Work in progress (revenue earned based on progress on projects but not yet billed)

I use the term 'relevant' to exclude those current assets that exist on the Balance Sheet but are unlikely to be easily convertible into cash.

There will often be a 'prepayments' balance, which represents any expenses that have been prepaid. For example, if you pay an annual insurance, software licence, rent or a membership in advance, this will be included in the prepayments balance. Usually you are unable to recover these payments, as you have contracted to that service for a period of time.

You may have a directors' loan account, with the intention to either repay it or declare a dividend to clear the balance. If the balance is expected to be repaid in more than 12 months, it will sit in long-term liabilities. If it is more likely to be cleared within 12 months, it will typically sit in current liabilities. In order to understand the value of current assets that are easily convertible into cash, you will need to be realistic about whether any directors' loan accounts sitting in current assets are going to be repaid to the company in the short term.

In addition to these examples, there is also a chance that your accountant has classed a balance as a current asset incorrectly! They may not have taken the time (or lacked sufficient information) to verify that a certain asset was not convertible for more than 12 months.

You can see how misleading this calculation can be if you purely run it based on the information in the Balance Sheet, so take the time to get the appropriate information and work with someone who understands accounting to verify that it is an accurate reflection of the financial position.

Analyzing the calculation

Once you have reliable figures for current assets and liabilities, you can run the calculations:

Current assets minus current liabilities = working capital

This provides the monetary value of working capital and hopefully it comes out positive! If not, the business is starved of cash and cannot meet its short-term obligations, let alone invest in growth.

This can also be expressed as a ratio, known as the current ratio:

Current assets divided by current liabilities

You need this to be at least '1' to be capable of settling short-term liabilities out of current assets. A better benchmark is '2x', meaning you have twice as many liquid assets as short-term liabilities. This gives breathing room and the ability to make investments that improve or grow the company without putting the cash in jeopardy.

Provide for the worst case

The current ratio is a great measure for ensuring the business has enough cash to meet its current obligations, but it neglects the fact that other commitments will soon be arriving. As an agency, you will have commitments every month that are not accounted for in the Balance Sheet because this sheet is a snapshot at a point in time. For example, if you look at a Balance Sheet dated 30th June, it will not show any of the expenses that are yet to be billed or incurred for activities in July, the largest one typically being salaries.

Another helpful measure of cash health is therefore to look at what would happen if all customers stopped paying and you were left to fund the business out of existing cash. The rule of thumb is to carry three to six months of overheads in cash. Obviously, there is a big difference in the value between three and six months. If your business is reliant on a few customers making up a large proportion of its revenue, aim for nearer to six. If revenues are diluted across many customers, then you carry less risk and therefore you might be satisfied with a ratio nearer to three.

Enhanced: Bringing facts into the figures: Creating a budget for your digital agency – what not to overlook

Figure 4.2. The budget building process

1.	Consider each type of revenue in isolation – Projects, retainers, one off.
2.	Increasing staff also increases equipment, software, office, employer's tax and pension costs.
3.	Budgets are not the same as targets. You can aim higher, but you should plan for what can be expected.
4.	Go beyond the financials – look at the drivers of the business.
5.	Lock the budget for the year and then assess whether a re-forecast is required after each financial quarter end.
6.	Involve your team – get different team members to feed into the parts that they work in.

Source: Paul Barnes, MAP

Case Study: An agency running out of cash

This agency in particular needed to keep a close eye on their cash position. For context, this agency had revenues of just over £5 million, with around 30 staff, award winning and very well respected in their sector.

The agency was going through a difficult phase where they were loss making, as client projects were pausing and business just generally slowed down. The business owners then decided to focus internally on their operational functions;

in doing so they had a drop in revenue, therefore less cash flowing into the business.

Alongside this they invested in their team and their operational structures and subsequently more cash was flowing out of the business. With this combination, the agency found itself in a situation where cash became tight. Tax payments were starting to be missed, negotiations with contractors were having to be made and even salary payments were now becoming a struggle.

Now imagine the stress of all the above and not having visibility or even an idea of what the cash balance figure meant, not knowing precisely what payments are coming up, what cash is coming in and most importantly how you're going to get out of this predicament. Or just maybe even worse having a forecast that isn't accurate or reliable, providing false information – now that's also another issue this agency faced. At the same time, the forecast they were using was overly complex and did not contain the correct information and so fluctuated unpredictably.

This client then engaged with MAP and started on their journey to become financially mature.

We clearly had to prioritize cash in this situation and so our team spent hours scrutinizing the cash flow of the business. It seems so simple – it's just cash coming in and out, right?

In this case, we had a lot of things to consider to pull the forecast together:

- Multiple revenue streams – billing at different points, with different payment terms for different clients.

- Revenue deposits – the agency was holding cash that they were yet to produce the work for, meaning a lower inflow of future cash for work being produced.
- Multiple contractors with different payment terms that were contributing significantly to the ongoing contracts.
- A large team where their salary payments potentially fluctuate each month, with sick leave, holidays and statutory payments, then the related PAYE liabilities.
- Dozens of subscriptions (which, without noticing, had built up incredibly fast).
- Loan repayments, and now payment plans with HMRC.

We spent a lot of time with the client understanding the business, trying to unpick their old forecast, revising months and months of bank statements to predict payment patterns and started compiling all the information into a new sheet. This resulted in a simple summary spreadsheet that contained all of this data – simply meaning the output was easily interpreted and decisions could confidently be made.

Now before we started using this forecast for making decisions, we went through the assumptions of the forecast with a fine tooth comb to make sure the business owners were on the same page with how we pulled this together. Assumptions is the key word here with this type of forecast and it is extremely important that everyone using it, whether it be updating or reading, is aligned with the basis of the forecast and the purpose. We therefore also produced a separate document detailing exactly where each piece of information had come from.

While all of this was going on, the cash obviously didn't miraculously pick up because that's not how this works. We did however start making more appropriate decisions when making supplier payments and the most important observation the forecast highlighted was that the agency was soon to become cash flow insolvent and we needed to resolve this quickly. They had a large VAT bill soon approaching, a quarterly rent payment on top of the ongoing payments that needed to be met, and we realized we needed funding immediately.

Then comes the next hurdle: how much do we need? How long do we need it for? How much can we afford to pay in interest? Imagine we got a loan at this point thinking it would relieve short-term pressure but was to be soon hit with a large repayment schedule with huge interest rates – this wouldn't help this would just delay the inevitable.

To prevent this, our team again spent a considerable amount of time scenario planning, using our finance forecast we had built by this point combined with running through multiple scenarios in our cash flow forecast: potential overdrafts; HMRC payment plans, funding applications, different interest rates, different repayment periods, different borrowing amounts. Beside us having to do this to make an informed decision we also needed to do this to prove to the funding company we would actually be able to meet the loan repayments – it's not so simple just walking into a bank and requesting a large loan without some substantial evidence that this is needed and can afford to repay.

In the end we managed to get the funding required, we held back paying people where appropriate and negotiated payment plans where possible, all while keeping a very close eye on the cash flow forecast to make sure we weren't deviating too much and if we were, understanding exactly what had caused it.

The agency is now cash healthy and is in the process of recovering from this stressful time. This wasn't down to luck or winging it; this was down to hours and hours of understanding the business, collating a lot of data and presenting it in a way to make informed decisions that consequently saved the business.

How do I secure funding for my business?

Here's the thought process to follow if the idea of raising finance is on your mind.

1. **Do you have a funding requirement?** It may seem like an obvious first step, but it's common to ask the question and get an unsure answer. Most service-based businesses can be grown organically if you're winning work that is being priced correctly and generating cash by having the right financial systems and processes in place. That being said, there are always exceptions where your particular aspirations may require a cash injection. It could be for anything from working capital, the development of products, to investing in the team or a particular marketing strategy.

   Your finance forecast is the way to cut through the confusion and know for sure if you do have a funding requirement. By mapping your scenario into a three-way forecast showing your P&L Report, Balance Sheet and cash flow, you know for sure if there's a requirement. It becomes factual and no longer based on a gut feeling, which allows the decision to be made more confidently. The last thing you want to do is raise finance to paper over the cracks. Often if you have a cash flow problem it's actually a profitability problem. If you find yourself looking to bring in some cash to cover losses, be sure to be fixing the source of the problem at the same time – otherwise it's a slippery slope.

2. **How do I go about it?** If you've built a finance forecast and it's demonstrating a need for a certain level of cash, the next step is to consider the best source of funding and that's split into two very different categories – equity and debt. If you go down the route of equity finance, you'll be bringing a cash investment into your business in exchange for shares and diluting your existing shareholding. For that reason, it's important to ensure that it's 'smart money' and that the investor is bringing something to the table other than just the cash. There will be people out there who have been on the same journey before and can bring expert guidance or a bank of useful contacts. You want to make sure that if

you're giving away 10% of your business, your retained 90% is worth more than 100% would be without them. Typical sources include friends and family, business contacts, online platforms, brokers and EIS (Enterprise Investment Schemes).

The other more common funding type is debt finance where you borrow cash to be paid back at a future date, usually with interest added. It's more popular as it tends to be easily accessible and less of a commitment. An overdraft with your existing bank is usually the first port of call, followed by credit cards, fixed repayment loans or invoice/asset finance. The trade-off is often that unless you're an established business with a strong Balance Sheet then personal guarantees by the directors can be required. It can also be costly in terms of initial fees and interest, so the decision to be made is whether that cost is outweighed by the progress it would allow you and the business to make.

3. **What next?** It's a genuine part of many business models for funding to be required in order for the goals to be hit. The key takeaway is to make sure the right questions are being asked; it's based on facts and not gut feelings, and that it's not being brought in to paper over the cracks of a struggling business.

The British Business Bank's survey showed that businesses only allow seven days to find the finance they need; spend just one hour researching possible providers and 80% apply to a single lender, typically their existing bank.[1]

---

[1] Almost 60% of SMEs spend less than an hour researching providers of lending:
https://assets.publishing.service.gov.uk/media/53eb6b73ed915d18880 0000c/SME-report_final.pdf
Around 70% of SMEs seeking loans approach only one provider, without considering alternatives; almost 90% then take out that loan with their main bank:

Don't leave it until the last minute to start a funding application. Give your business the time and leverage to secure the best deals available.

Here's a quick overview for how to be prepared for a funding application:

- Plan in advance, even if you don't think you have a requirement, you never know what opportunity might be around the corner; be ready to take advantage.
- Keep tabs on the macro environment and where interest rates are at so you can plan for better terms.
- The purpose is really important, make sure you are presenting to funders in a way where they can see you have clearly thought about how you will use the funds and how it is going to benefit your business (lenders want to be comfortable that you will repay).
- Track your personal and business credit score as lenders will look at a six-month average; if you want to access good rates you should try and maintain high scores.
- Look beyond just your bank; high street banks are retrenching whereas financial technology (fintechs) and challengers (e.g. Monzo, Starling, Tide) are lending more in the small- and medium-sized enterprises (SME) space.
- Understand what lenders want to see.
- Clear bank statements with no missed payments.

---

https://assets.publishing.service.gov.uk/media/53eb6b73ed915d188800000c/SME-report_final.pdf
More than half of SMEs (55%) would like to be funded within seven days:
www.ey.com/en_gl/insights/banking-capital-markets/the-five-step-journey-to-sme-banking-transformation
For working capital, the mean average period was 6.5 days (how soon before needing it is finance applied for):
www.british-business-bank.co.uk/sites/g/files/sovrnj166/files/2023-02/SME-Journey-Towards-Raising-Finance.pdf

- Good personal credit of directors or business.
- Well defined purpose for funds.
- Profitable with at least two sets of filed accounts.
- Low level of existing debt.
- Clear affordability (e.g. EBITDA of 1.25 × debt service costs).
- Willingness or ability to provide additional security.

Make sure you can provide the appropriate information; while it might take more time, it will help you find the right product and provider, ensuring you get a good deal.

EXTENDED

Chapter 5
Extended: Mature financial thinking

FINANCE IS AN essential function of any business, but it can also complete the leadership picture and enable the development of an increasingly sophisticated agency.

Employing more people just to bring in high-level skills is impractical and expensive, especially as priorities and challenges you face today are probably not going to be the same in six months' time. There is a point where appropriate skills are required on a more targeted project basis than a full-time, part-time or contracted arrangement.

Financial leadership

An independent and practical voice to challenge, uncover and deliver

Having the insight, interpretation and investigative skills of an experienced independent finance professional are important ones to be able to call upon when needed.

They can add immediate value to strategy and direction, but also to operational and commercial matters like processes, contract construction, profitability and providing a touchstone for the whole team. Recognizing the importance of financial leadership, acknowledges that the business needs access to experience and expertise in order to maintain sustainable growth.

I do worry that people put finance professionals on a pedestal at times. They see accounting and finance as so alien to them that they just need someone to take it off their plate. They don't have the training or patience themselves to process data and produce reports so they look to the people with the experience.

This makes sense. It takes at least six years of training, exams and hands on experience to become a chartered accountant, so people with these qualifications are trusted to do the work. They understand the technical aspects and how to get the data right. But data needs work to become useful information and presenting useful information is another skill.

One client that we started working with had three directors and one of them said that they had never understood the financial reports that were provided by our predecessor accountancy firm. They had been receiving those reports every month for three years!

People often don't speak up when they don't understand something because they are embarrassed they will look stupid. This only gets exacerbated the more time goes by because they are now admitting that they haven't been absorbing the information that the company is paying for.

Even when information is understood, it doesn't mean that the recipients will know what further questions to ask. While accounting is a science, finance is an art and it can be presented, interpreted and analyzed in many different ways. A great finance professional will adapt their approach to the business, its people and even the situation – you can't speak to someone whose business is failing the same way as you can to one that is flying.

So, if you are looking to bring financial expertise into your business, be that on an employed or contracted basis, take the time to truly understand the credentials of the people you are considering relying upon for the most crucial aspect of your business.

Here's a checklist for you to work through to check for suitability.

1. **Are they qualified?** As well as confidence in ability, qualifications also provide reassurance that a finance professional is properly governed. It comes as a shock to many that the accounting industry is by default unregulated. Anyone who is not a member of a regulated body is free to set up their own firm and it will be unregulated! It is a staggering reality that many business owners are unaware of. When a finance professional becomes a member of a regulated body, they have to undertake intensive training and examinations and prove their competence. They have to follow a code of ethics. They are then subjected to continuous professional development (CPD) to prove that they are keeping abreast of changes in regulation, for as long as they remain in practice. They are also regulated in their conduct, including a requirement to obtain certain levels of professional indemnity insurance to protect you from the advice they and/or their colleagues provide to you and your business. They are required to implement a formal complaints procedure for

when you are not satisfied that they have delivered the service that was sold to you.

There are several credible qualifications in the UK. The Association of Accounting Technicians (AAT) is a great start and pathway into the chartered bodies:
- Association of Chartered Certified Accountants (ACCA)
- Chartered Accountants Ireland (CAI)
- Chartered Institute of Management Accountants (CIMA)
- Chartered Institute of Public Finance and Accounting (CIPFA)
- ICAEW (Institute of Chartered Accountants in England and Wales)
- Institute of Chartered Accountants of Scotland (ICAS)

2. **Are they experienced in your sector?** According to the CCAB and CIMA (Appendix 3:6), there are more than 350,000 qualified accounting professionals in the UK. You are not in a position where you need to compromise working with someone that lacks experience advising other businesses that are similar to yours. There is a language in the digital sector and if you work with a finance professional that speaks that language, you are going to have more seamless and valuable conversations and support. There are also common KPIs, reporting and financial/operational technology in the digital sector that you want your finance people to be abreast of. Without this sector knowledge and experience, you will feel like it's the tail wagging the dog – as you will be the one coming up with all of the questions and ideas, despite paying for it! So check their track record of experience in your sector, not just what they tell you but what their website and online presence shows you and ideally speak to their existing clients to ask how they have similar businesses to yours.

3. **Do they fit with your culture?** I worry that culture is now seen incorrectly by too many as a happy place to work with

pool tables and bean bags. Every business does, and should, have a unique culture that encompasses the language used, the accepted behaviours, the risk profile and many other aspects. Do you and your team prefer information to be detailed or simple? Do you like to work at speed or take your time? Do you like directness or friendliness? There are no right or wrong answers here, just cultural differences that are important. If you find a finance partner that suits your culture, you will enjoy working with them more, have a longer tenure and ultimately achieve better results.

Making the best use of a finance partner

When you invest in working with a finance partner, you want to make sure you make the most of their skills. It's not just about listening and paying attention to their advice. Obviously that would be wise because they have a different skill to offer to your business and should be helping to identify your blind spots. This is not just about avoiding risk either; a good finance partner should be uncovering opportunities for the business to exploit. More on that later but I want to explain why I use the term finance *partner*. Not director/manager/controller because a finance professional should be someone that you and your business collaborate with. You work on ideas and execution together.

They are not the superheroes here to save the day; they are a partner who appreciates that you know more about your business than they ever will. You are the one fulfilling a passion to solve a need that you have identified in the market. You know the proposition, the customers and the culture better than they do and they have complementary skills that when combined mean that you exploit more opportunities and manage more of the risks.

If there is one thing to take away from this book more than anything else, it would be to partner with finance professionals rather than abdicate responsibility to them. If you are going to run a great business you can't avoid paying attention to the finances. Instead, I urge you to lean in to understanding your numbers and working with the right people to partner on your unique journey.

Voice of reason

Finance professionals are often labelled as the negative voice in the room, always focusing on risk and how to avoid it at all costs. It might be suggested that business owners (and any leadership team they might have) are positive people, focused on opportunities for growth and they fear that a finance professional is only going to find flaws in their plan and perhaps even quash their dreams. Not everyone is open to constructive feedback, and unfortunately, it holds them back in a big way.

I knew of a digital agency that was starting to struggle financially and I offered to spend some time with them. I could see from their trajectory that they were heading in the wrong direction and needed to think about coming up with a new plan to turn the tide. If they had agreed, we would have taken measures to slow down the decline while putting a turnaround plan in place. They didn't want to listen. They talked about a strong pipeline and that they just needed to convert a couple of big projects and they would be fine.

They got stuck in this cycle for years. I kept offering my time but it felt as though I was more concerned about their business than they were. I watched them crash into insolvency – their debts were spiralling and the losses continued. They needed to take drastic action but instead they got away with paying those who shouted loudest and ignored the wider problems. That business is on the verge of liquidation today. Its creditors and employees have been let down by poor financial management and the directors will likely be disqualified for wrongful trading (continuing to trade despite worsening their creditors' position).

Bravery is a key trait to start a business, but there is a line between being brave and being reckless. In this instance, they showed no respect for their obligations to pay their tax liabilities, their suppliers and to follow the law!

You have chosen to read this book so it is highly likely you have respect for your obligations as a director and welcome the opportunity to do good for your team, everyone you do business with and indeed, yourself.

Rather than viewing finance professionals as the negative voice, I see them as the voice of reason. They are not there just to put fright into you, but they are not paid just to pat you on the back either. They should listen, ask good questions and seek to properly understand your business so that they can provide valuable insight. Often it's about helping you and your team to explore to a deeper level and not make decisions based on surface level information and emotion.

You might feel as though your business should be extending its service range because you've seen a need from one or more customers for something that you don't currently offer. A good finance partner won't tell you it's a bad idea that will cause too much distraction. They will say, 'Great, let's explore that further.' They respect that you are the one on the front line, in the market and in the know about what customers want. Every business needs to be focused on market needs. Without that, no finance expert is going to be worth investing in.

Exploring an idea means partnering with all of the people that can provide insight – customer need, margin, growth potential, seasonality, operational complexity, skills match and many more considerations – in order to fully appraise the opportunity. Then when the decision is made to press ahead or kill the idea, everyone not only understands the decision but moves forward full of vigour. Even ruling something out feels good because strategy is often as much about being clear about all the things your business doesn't do as well as what it does.

So don't work with finance professionals who bring the energy of the room down, find a finance partner who you can trust to be the voice of reason. Here's a word from David Arden, Finance Partner at MAP, about his experience partnering with a client to improve financial confidence and performance.

Financial leadership in practice

The client is an established business of 15 years, which more recently has seen significant year on year revenue growth up to ~£10m. As is often the case, it was coming with an increased cost base and not showing itself in the most important number, the bottom line profit. There were more clients, more projects, more people and more headaches, but the directors and shareholders were not seeing the deserved results of all the hard work.

In fact, the growth in itself was starting to put significant financial pressure on the business, whereby the nature of the project work and the corporate client base meant the cash flow, and therefore the future solvency of the business, was becoming a real concern.

The incumbent finance function was in need of a refresh, with the existing combination of two employees internally, an external finance director (FD) and finance controller (FC), plus an external accountant not delivering what was required.

A timeline was agreed whereby a finance partner (FP) taking a seat at the monthly Board meetings would come in the future but was not put in place initially. The first priority was to overhaul the finance function itself, so that the data and reporting was in place to give the Board every chance of making the right decisions throughout the turnaround plan. The previous reporting was complex with an overload of data and numbers but was not focusing on the right areas and fundamentally was not trusted.

At the same time the FP began thoroughly understanding the business model, to identify what the key drivers were that would result in the required financial outcomes. A re-budget was done, making it clear to all involved what the minimum financial performance was that would see the business through this period and be able to continue trading. Costs were reviewed and anything not adding value to the business was challenged. The revenue potential of the existing team was increased through a review of the rate card and increase in billable time across the team, with typically non-billable staff being targeted to contribute each month. The sales and marketing team understood specifically what needed to be won and when. Communication to the wider team was essential at this point. They had to be aware that change was needed, as it is their contributions every day that will deliver that change, but not feel concerned about their roles and livelihoods.

In any service business, its most significant cost is its people. In this example, the team represented one of the strongest in the UK within the niche that it operates – real leaders in the space that the business had worked hard to recruit, develop and retain. Plan A was therefore not to have to change that team, but nonetheless the scenarios were played out. People decisions are often the hardest ones to make as they come with relationships and emotions – but the lines in the sand were agreed by which those decisions would need to be considered if it was required for the survival of the business.

When the FP then started attending the monthly Board meeting – the finance report was always first on the agenda – and was delivered with the right balance of empathy to appreciate the personal position of those involved and the mental challenges they were going through, combined with the honesty required to share that the business was under significant pressure.

Throughout the rest of the monthly Board meetings, the FP was on hand to bring commercial challenges and tie the contributions of the other directors who were the experts in their respective areas back to the implications on the numbers. Outside of the Board meetings, the change in mindset of the directors to now running a performance focused business started to permeate itself into the conversations that were being had with the wider team. Relationships were built between the FP and the other senior team members in the business to further aid bridging the gap between sales, marketing, people, operations and finance.

The survival of the business was a multi-pronged attack, with profitability improvement and close cash management the two priorities. Whenever there was an improvement identified – whether a quick win or a slower burn – it was considered how this can be applied to future processes and the commercial terms with clients to reduce the risk of the same scenario reappearing in future. At the same time, funding was secured through agreed support from creditors to give the required window of cash flow for the incremental improvements to gain traction.

The experience of the FP meant that they could guide the directors through what was important to focus on and what was not. In business, there will always be issues and things that can be improved, but not all can be done at once making prioritization the real skill. Any longer term initiatives were put on the back burner to return to at a later date.

The support from the FP meant that the CEO and the operations director (OD) in particular could focus on what they do best, trusting that they had the right plan in place with the accountability and guidance required to see it through.

David Arden, Finance Partner at MAP

So make sure you work with someone in finance who has your best interests at heart. Of course they need to be technically qualified and experienced, but that's a given.

Mapping the strategy

Providing clarity and focus on strategic direction

Mapping the strategy should be a defined process that provides an opportunity to stand back from the day to day and take a dispassionate view of the business and personal ambitions of the business owners.

Once the direction is properly understood, with documented clear goals, then the mechanics of the business can be engineered to deliver. This should respect every aspect of the business: high-level financials that lead into looking at client numbers, honing the service offering and the make up and skills within the team.

Together it should assemble a credible story for the whole organization.

Start with the end in mind. When you imagine the perfect business to own, what does it look like? How much profit is it making? What does the team shape and size look like? What's your role, if any? Take your time answering these questions because once you decide, you are going to commit your focus and resources towards that goal, so it better be one that matters to you!

Having a strategy is uplifting. Not only does it help you to think about all the things you are going to do, equally it helps you to realize a lot of the things you no longer need to worry about. Executing a plan is challenging enough. Trying to build a business without a plan is on a whole new level, fraught with stress, indecision and general chaos as every new idea feels like it needs exploring. There are endless opportunities out there for you but try to go after too many of them and you never achieve any of them.

How much money do I need?

I recently asked Adam Downes, Financial Planner at Pura Vida, to talk us through the process of working out how much money we need to live our best lives. Here's what he had to say.

An interview with Adam Downes, Financial Planner at Pura Vida

I get asked this question in one format or another more than a hundred times a year. Everyone wants to know, are we going to be ok? As annoying as it is, I answer this question with another question: 'Well, how do you want to live, now and in the future?'

If you really think about, I mean, really think about how your ideal life looks like for you and your family, it goes a long way to being able to start answering our big question.

There are two things that I find most commonly stop us from living a life more aligned with what makes us happy: time and money. We know our time on this earth is finite, I say on almost a daily basis I don't have enough time. I don't think there's an easy answer to this problem unfortunately, but personally I am working towards being more deliberate with the time I have.

What we can do is remove the barrier of money. As a starting point, we need to think about the cost of what we want to do now, versus the cost of what we want to do in the future:

- Ongoing living costs: We need to pay for things like the mortgage, utilities and food, right?

- Ongoing enjoyment expenditure: How do you like to spend your spare time? Whatever your thing is, where is your money best spent to make you happy?
- Annual holidays: Holidays can be really important; how would your year look if you doubled your holiday budget?
- One-off living costs: How often do you need to replace the car? Do you have any work planned on your house?
- One-off enjoyment: Think bucket list ideas, recreation and future celebrations.
- Once you have an idea of how you live on an ongoing basis, it gives you the foundation of a budget. If you multiply that number by 30, 40 or 50 depending on how many years you might live, it turns into a rather big number. Add to it the one-off costs and that number grows even larger.

Once you go through this exercise, you can then start to answer the question: how much money do I need? And perhaps more importantly, do I have enough? For most people who are still working, the answer is a hard NO!

That doesn't mean we need to panic. Personally, I am many years away from having enough.

What is important is to have a robust, reliable plan to have enough. We know life can change quickly but I do encourage anyone reading this to plan for the future. Your future self will thank you. A plan is not just about the long term – what do you have planned for the next 12 months and what can you do in the next five years?

Enjoy the journey, we don't know how much time we have.

Adam Downes, Financial Planner at Pura Vida

Not always about the end goal

I've seen a lot of people screw up their businesses because they were following a dream that wasn't their own. The consultant tells them they can grow their business multiple fold with the right plan. They are sold the dream of a well-oiled machine that allows the owner to step back and watch the cash pour in. They show them how to build a business that will have acquirers fighting over each other in a bidding war.

The concept of the lifestyle business gets belittled in favour of the *build to sell* mentality. Lifestyle for many means following a hobby – effectively using a business as a vehicle to exercise their craft. It will never be worth anything and the owner will be wedded to it for its lifetime.

The truth is that most people are going to be happier with a lifestyle business. Less people to manage, less customers to worry about, generally less headaches and a better quality of life. Those that have scaled a business often bemoan the feeling of a loss of purpose, explaining that they could just be running 'any old business', as they feel so far removed from the core of what the business is about.

The real kicker is that many of the businesses that have scaled are producing a lower income for the business owner than it did when it was smaller! The increasing non-chargeable resources have suffocated profit margins and it's a long and gruelling road to the other side where it hopefully feels worth it all.

You've probably heard the story of the fisherman but it goes like this:[1]

> An American investment banker was at the pier of a small coastal Mexican village when a small boat with just one fisherman docked. Inside the small boat were several large yellowfin tuna. The American complimented the Mexican on the quality of his fish and asked how long it took to catch them.
>
> The Mexican replied: 'Only a little while'. The American then asked why didn't he stay out longer and catch more fish? The Mexican said he had enough to support his

---

[1] *The famous parable is often referred to as 'The Banker and the Fisherman' or 'The Mexican Fisherman' demonstrating two sides: simplicity and gratitude versus blind ambition.*

family's immediate needs. The American then asked: 'But what do you do with the rest of your time?'

The Mexican fisherman said: 'I sleep late, fish a little, play with my children, take siestas with my wife, Maria, stroll into the village each evening where I sip wine, and play guitar with my amigos. I have a full and busy life.'

The American scoffed: 'I am a Harvard MBA and could help you. You should spend more time fishing and with the proceeds buy a bigger boat. With the proceeds from the bigger boat, you could buy several boats, eventually you would have a fleet of fishing boats. Instead of selling your catch to a middleman you would sell directly to the processor, eventually opening your own cannery. You would control the product, processing and distribution. You would need to leave this small coastal fishing village and move to Mexico City, then LA and eventually New York City, where you will run your expanding enterprise.'

The Mexican fisherman asked: 'But, how long will this all take?'

To which the American replied: '15–20 years.'

'But what then?' asked the Mexican.

The American laughed and said: 'That's the best part. When the time is right you would announce an initial public offering (IPO) and sell your company stock to the public and become very rich; you would make millions!'

'Millions – then what?'

The American said: 'Then you would retire. Move to a small coastal fishing village where you would sleep late, fish a little, play with your kids, take siestas with your wife, stroll to the village in the evenings where you could sip wine and play your guitar with your amigos.'

So, do you want a high-performance, high-scale company that you can exit for a life-changing amount of money, or do you want a highly profitable lifestyle business that gives you freedom, fulfilment and fun? There is no better answer – the only thing that matters is that it suits you and the life that you want to live.

Often those that are more lifestyle oriented find that they are much closer to what they are seeking. There is a goal setting exercise that you can work through to help you to clearly understand the size and shape of business that is required to give you the outcomes that you want.

Figure 5.1. Goal setting tool

1. **Calculate a fair salary for your role in the business.** If you stepped away from the business and you needed to be replaced, what would the business need to budget?
   You are likely to still be playing a crucial role in the operation of your company.
   If you hired someone to do your role, they would be paid a healthy salary to do so. You should therefore be receiving that salary yourself while you continue to deliver that role. We'll call this your commercial salary.
   See the link in Appendix 2 for guidance on benchmark director salaries.
   At our last look, the benchmark salary for a Managing Director (MD) was £75k.

2. **Calculate a healthy return for you as a shareholder.** What do you want your business to pay you as a shareholder (or an investor)?
   In addition to the commercial salary, how much additional money would you like to take out of the business – you need to get rewarded for all of the risk and effort that you've contributed as a shareholder.
   Over time you may look to step away from the day-to-day activities of your business and rely 100% on the return of being a shareholder.

3. **Calculate the return for other shareholders.** What do you want your business to pay any other investors?
   Think about any shareholders outside of your family. If there are any, they need a return proportionate to their shareholding.

4. **Calculate a level of profits to retain.** What profit do you want to keep in the business each year?
   Retained profit is the absolute bottom line for the year after interest, depreciation, tax and dividends.
   As a starter, you might want to ensure you build six months of overhead in retained profit.

5. **Calculate the current overheads.** What are the business overheads, excluding your salary?
   Overheads are the fixed costs that it takes to run your business, which includes your team and office but excludes your own salary, dividends and corporation tax.

6. **Calculate the extra resources needed.** What additional costs are required to operate and grow?
   You may feel that you'll need to invest – this may be growing the team or spending more on sales and marketing.

7. **Calculate gross margin.** What is the expected gross margin?
   The % of the revenue left after any direct cost associated with each £ of revenue.

8. **Calculate the value of a typical customer or project.** What is the annual revenue expected from your target typical customer or project?

9. **Calculate rate card.** Target rate £ per hour
   You may have a rate card that you charge clients.

10. **Calculate utilization.** What is your team's efficiency/utilization? What percentage of the total team's hours are billable?

Once you have the answers to each of these questions, copy them into the 'Goal Setting Tool' in Appendix 2. Your desired

P&L Report will be calculated along with the required number of clients and team members, so that you can see what the right size and shape business is to meet your goals.

This is often an enlightening exercise as it provides clarity on what you *really* want, not necessarily what you thought you wanted. Often, it will show that your ideal size and shape business is not as out of reach as you expected.

Obviously, you still need to work on achieving the purpose that you want to fight for, your role in the business, and generally being fulfilled, but knowing what the financial model needs to look like is a huge step.

The number of clients is also only part of the equation because the quality of clients and your team's relationship with them is equally important if you are going to sustain this ideal business model.

I have yet to meet an agency that doesn't want to provide the maximum value it can to its clients. Most of us set up a business because we believe there is a better way of serving a market, so giving value is firmly rooted in our DNA.

We want to deliver a great service because seeing results for your clients, and getting positive feedback from them, is what makes us feel better than anything else. When you do that you increase retention of clients and how much they spend with you, you get referrals, have a happier workforce and generally feel like you have something that can scale.

Of course, giving value is not enough, you need to be receiving value back. It's no good if your clients think you're the best thing ever to happen to them but you're broke.

The value exchange has to be two way for your business to thrive. The vital ingredient for receiving value back is profitability. You can't build a business without it. If your client is losing you money then no matter how good everything else is, you can't sustain that relationship.

Best and worst clients

In order to achieve that two-way value exchange, you need to find win–win relationships in your client base. When you think of your best and worst clients you probably think in terms of how much they value what you do.

The best ones are constantly thanking you and telling you how pleased they are with your service. The worse ones are regularly complaining, asking for more, but complaining about the price.

When you think about those best clients, are they really the best for you in terms of the two-way value exchange described above? In my experience, the best clients value you so much that they gradually take a stranglehold of your team.

You likely have four types of clients.

Lose–win clients

They have your mobile numbers in their phone book and don't think twice about disturbing you in the evenings and at weekends. They add you into their slack channels and expect almost instant responses.

They praise what a great job you've done and swiftly follow up with a request of 'if you could just…'. They expect you to travel out and see them and for you to fund the cost.

They want to be able to come and see you whenever they like, again using your time without paying for it. These clients win because they get everything they want from your relationship. They have the experience and skills of an in-house team at their fingertips but without the stress and cost. You've taken that on for them! You will likely make very little profit on these clients.

Lose–lose clients

The clients at the bottom of the list are those that, however hard you try, never seem to be pleased. They ask for more from you but complain about the cost. They pick at the niggly issues and quickly forget about the more impactful things that you've delivered to them.

Instead of focusing on outcomes, they are bogging you and themselves down by analyzing the time you've spent and the inputs. They are not satisfied that they are getting what they paid for and you are losing money by continuing with them as a client.

Win–win clients

These are usually found somewhere in the middle of your best and worst clients. They are pleased that what they receive from you is value for the money they spend.

They thank you for doing a good job and see your role in their bigger picture. They have shared expectations with you about what should be delivered for the fees they pay and they don't try to squeeze you for everything they can. They are therefore profitable, durable and enjoyable to work with.

Win–lose clients

These are the clients that make you a healthy profit but you are not delivering results for them. They don't complain too much yet but at some point, they will become aware that they are not getting a good deal and will quickly move into one of the categories above.

Whatever size your agency, it's likely that you will have clients in all three of the main categories. Your goal is to morph your client base into win–win only clients.

The lose–win clients are usually capable of being win–win clients. It is often our own doing that they have become too demanding because we've not set the boundaries of the relationship.

By taking ownership of the problem, you can apologize for not being clearer on how they should best interact with your team. Approaching it this way builds trust and openness as most of those clients want to be good clients and have a healthy two-way relationship and they will when they are shown how.

Be very careful not to talk about the need to 'have time to service other clients' as the reason why you're addressing the relationship. They don't care about your other clients. They want to feel cared for, like you're determined to get results together with them, almost like they are your only client. They just need educating on where the goalposts are so that they can play fairly.

If they want more than you are currently charging for, and you are happy to do the things they ask, then quote for it. Give them a quote for keeping the service the same (at an increased price) and a quote for keeping the price the same (with reduced services) and they have options. This is really important because your clients don't want to feel forced into paying more, so give them the option to keep paying the same, but with clear boundaries.

The lose–lose clients are very rarely capable of becoming win–win clients. They have to improve the way they work with you *and* pay more. If they've been difficult so far it is unlikely they are going to change and even more unlikely that they will pay the increased fee.

People talk about 'sacking' your worst clients but I find that disrespectful and uncomfortable. It's much more amicable for you both if you can help to direct them to another service provider who better supports their needs – a smaller agency, freelancer, perhaps a specialist in their industry. Before you refer them elsewhere, there is nothing to be lost in sending them a proposal that represents how you need things to work. If they accept then you have new guidelines and a price that gives you what you need to make it work. If they don't, then you positively refer them to the other provider, not by apologizing but by enthusiastically explaining to them that you have a better option for them with a provider that you can endorse.

Building an agency by design and not default

Most agencies are started by a designer/developer/marketer who is good at what they do and go out alone. You start to win clients and take on staff and before you know it you have a growing business. The problem is that the more you take on, the more you need.

The more clients you have, the more staff you need and then the more stuff you take on, the more you rely on keeping and winning clients. If you don't design the agency to be the one you want, you will end up growing by default – and that compromise in quality of clients and staff will lead to frustration and burnout.

Building an agency by design means figuring out what type of clients you want, what price they will pay, what you want them to buy, how you will attract them with your marketing, the type of people that you want to work for you, what values you will run the business by, how you will deliver the work efficiently and profitably, etc.

In a word, this is simply what strategy is – designing your dream agency and then going and building it. Once you're clear on what you want, everything else has to go. If you don't make the difficult decisions now, they only get harder and cause you more problems.

Mapping the strategy: Using the data to light up performance

Use a structured process to ensure you are creating a truly integrated vision and strategy. The MAP way is designed exclusively for digital agencies and incorporates:

- Personal goals
- Business goals

- Financial position
- Services and their profitability
- Team and their efficiencies
- Financial systems

🚀 Specialist services

Accessing appropriate professional services

A maturing agency will require access to professional advice in key areas as it continues to grow and develop. Typically, these are more front and centre in the minds of Board members and are strategic matters that require a level of technical or financial expertise to execute.

These can be far ranging, for example, incentives, share option schemes and employee benefits as part of a wider plan to attract, retain and reward staff. Or preparing and marketing the business for sale, buying out an existing shareholder or acquiring a complementary business.

These matters need to be coordinated by a professional as they are often processes that can derail without guidance and proper regulatory knowledge.

Credit scores

Credit scores are used by many but the most frequent examples are:

- **Prospective customers**: to check the resilience of your business – they don't want to sign up to work with a company only for that company to fail and they are left without a key supplier.
- **Suppliers**: to ascertain what credit terms they can extend to you and even whether they can trust you to pay at all!
- **Lenders**: to assess track record of settling debt to support their decision in lending to you now or in the future.

If you are looking to finance the business at any stage, the lender has to make a risk versus reward assessment based on credit scores and general financial health. These factors will drive the decision on the rates offered (the higher the perceived risk, the higher the rates) and indeed whether they are willing to lend to your business at all.

The credit bureaus that assign companies with the credit scores do so based on information they have access to via Companies House and other financial institutions, for example, current and past lending that a business has used and how well it has kept to its repayments.

Those bureaus don't see any of the financial information that is not publicly available through Companies House or these financial institutions. This can be a real problem where your last filed accounts are outdated. Even if you feel that the financial position was healthy at that point, the complex algorithms that the bureaus use to calculate credit scores could put more weight on any single data point, which could work against you.

At MAP, we work with these bureaus to provide more up-to-date information that isn't publicly available. We do this by providing year to date financial reports and/or explaining the practical reasons behind any weaknesses on the financial records, such as failed payments that are no fault of our clients.

We actually had an experience at MAP a few years ago where our bank rejected some forms that they had asked us for. They didn't like one of the signatures because it didn't display clearly on the scanned image. Incredibly they blocked our account! This was a major issue because it was our main trading account for paying all suppliers and staff. We quickly got it sorted and no one was left out of pocket but because it automatically cancelled all of our outgoing direct debits and even though we settled them manually the same day, 'default payments' were listed on our records. This then fed through to the credit bureaus and our score dropped from 100/100 to 49/100 overnight.

We didn't need funding so it wasn't affecting us that way but as an accountancy firm and outsourced finance function who preach about good financial management, we were not best pleased. We opened a dialogue with the credit bureaus and provided the explanation of what had happened with the bank and they immediately corrected our credit score back to full marks.

As if the stress of the bank blocking our account wasn't enough, we then had the added pain of witnessing our credit score tumble. Hopefully this serves as an example of the many trivial matters that could cause your credit score to be affected, often through no fault of your own.

So to protect your reputation, cost of borrowing and credit worthiness, I urge you to have a system in place to monitor your credit score and never take it as given if it's not putting your business in a favourable light. Work with the bureaus to lift it up.

Who will take this business forward for me?

If you are serious about scaling your business, you can't do it alone. You will need other leaders and managers to provide expertise and focus on each of the core areas of the business.

Key people at this level have significant expectations both in the short and long term. They want to be paid well for the role they carry out and they want to be rewarded for growing the business and helping you to achieve your goals.

If you reach this point in your journey, it is a delicate matter that needs dealing with properly. I have seen too many business owners being overly generous only for it to backfire. As someone who has started a business, the thought of being offered the chance to benefit from the growth of the company seems like an incredible opportunity in your mind. Not everyone else sees it that way. Human beings are complex. We all have different backgrounds, experiences and battle scars.

One key employee of a client's business was offered a very handsome opportunity to acquire shares in the company with no financial outlay. It seemed like a given to the founders that this employee would bite their hand off at the opportunity – all to gain and nothing to lose. To their surprise, the employee reacted very differently. He stated that it 'felt very capitalist' and that he felt uncomfortable being part of it.

When you've built a business up from the ground, those people that have been on the journey with you from an early stage don't necessarily see the growth as positively as you might. They often crave the simplicity and beauty of the early days when it felt more like a family than a business. They start to miss the simplicity of being able to make decisions instantly, have meetings in the pub and see and hear everything in the office. They were probably your star employee at one point and probably operated with a very fluid role.

As the business grew, it required them to fulfil more specific requirements and be accountable for the not insignificant salary that they get paid. There is so much emotion built up in these relationships and everyone is different. You can't be sure how they see things, however well you know them, because people are complex and they change their views over time.

Before you start building incentive packages, make sure that you consider the drivers for each individual respectively. What motivates one person is not necessarily the same as what motivates another. One might be happy to make more sacrifices and take more risk for a higher potential reward, whereas others might prefer to be fairly compensated to perform a role without the additional stress.

One consideration could be to reward individuals with equity in the business. This can either be an immediate transaction or the option to acquire shares in the future. If they acquire shares right away then they instantly benefit from the rights attached to those shares –

typically the right to dividends, to capital or to vote on company matters. An option, on the other hand, provides the individual with the right to acquire shares at a future date. When that date arrives, they can choose whether or not to exercise that option.

In both cases, you have key decisions to make about how much equity to offer, what rights to attach to the shares and what payment, if any, you expect the individual to make to acquire them.

How much equity should I offer?

In order to answer this question, think about the *value* that you want to retain first, before considering percentages. For the value that you want to extract in terms of dividends and capital, what can you afford to sacrifice?

If you want to take £200,000 of dividends per year and the business is expecting to make £300,000 of retained profits, that suggests that you can afford to offer 33% of the dividends to new shareholders. If you want to gain £2m of capital upon exiting the business and the business is expected to be sold for £2.5m, then this suggests you can only afford to offer 20% of the capital.

Issuing 20% or 33% of the share capital doesn't necessarily mean that those individuals automatically get that same percentage of voting rights. You can alter the voting rights to be independent of the percentage of shares being issued.

If you are offering share options that can only be exercised in the event of a company sale, then voting rights and dividends are irrelevant. Only the capital proceeds matter in that instance.

If you are offering 'shares today' then the voting, dividends and capital are all very important considerations. You also need to think about the value you are offering now as well as how that will change as the business grows.

How share options work in practice

You can probably already understand some of the reasons that share options are so common:

- You don't have to give any of the current value away.
- You can assign objectives to the options so that they are tied to company performance.
- You don't need to consider dividend or voting rights if they are tied to an exit.

There are also considerable tax benefits available for HMRC approved share options. Where these HMRC criteria are met, the individual avoids a tax charge arising at the time of the option being granted.

Let's look at an illustrative example.

> **Share options in action**
>
> An employee is granted an option to acquire 10 shares in three years' time at no cost to them, with a current value of £100,000. Three years later they are worth £250,000.
>
> If this option is wrapped within an HMRC approved share option scheme, then the employee avoids income tax and national insurance on the £100,000 of value being gifted to them.
>
> If that individual is a higher rate taxpayer, that's 40%* income tax plus 2% national insurance. 42% × £100,000 = £42,000 that they would have had to have funded out of their own pocket for the privilege of a share option that gives them no immediate cash!
>
> When the employee eventually receives capital for their shares upon an exit, they will usually pay capital gains tax on the growth in the share value from the date of exercise to the date of disposal. Capital gains tax is usually a much lower

> rate than income tax and if at least two years passes between the granting of the share options and the employee disposing of their shares, they may be entitled to pay the lower rate of capital gains tax, subject to the provisions of Business Asset Disposal Relief (formerly Entrepreneurs Relief).
>
> The company also benefits from corporation tax savings – the difference between the market value of the shares on exercise and the amount paid by the employee is a deduction from taxable profits. In this example that's £250,000 less NIL**, so a £250,000 saving at the company's rate of corporation tax.
>
> *In today's legislation, they would also likely lose their personal allowance and move into the additional rate of tax so the tax charge could quite possibly be even higher.*
> ***NIL** because in this example the employee didn't pay anything for the shares.*

Essentially, an HMRC approved share option scheme is going to incentivize key employees to grow the value of the company because in turn they are growing the value of the shares that they have the option to acquire, with no financial outlay and on a very tax effective basis for when they eventually sell those shares.

It can be a really effective way to prepare for your succession and build a motivated leadership team to take the business forward.

Just give yourself plenty of time to work through the process and get it right, and don't disclose too much to your team members and get their expectations up before you have ironed out the details.

Growth shares

Another way to retain the value that you have built in the business so far, while giving others the incentive to grow it further, is via the use of growth shares.

Growth shares allow you to offer shares immediately, therefore avoiding the share options process. The shares that are issued are typically a separate class from those that you own, in order to allow different rights. This means you can offer dividends and capital beyond specified thresholds.

Let's say the business currently has £1m of capital value and generates £150,000 of retained earnings per year.

You could issue a new type of growth share that pays:

- Capital when the business is sold for a sum above the £1m hurdle.
- Dividends when retained earnings in any year exceed the £150,000 hurdle.

This approach means you are not diluting your current value and instead sharing in the future growth.

If you have no near term plans to sell the business then a share option scheme that vests on an exit might be near worthless. A growth share issue on the other hand gives those who are instrumental in building the business the instant opportunity to benefit from its continued growth.

In summary, a share option scheme works well when you want to incentivize someone to stay with the business and grow it further but you don't feel comfortable issuing those shares today.

If you are comfortable with issuing shares today, then growth shares are a plausible option. You do however need to work on clauses in the contract for if that person either leaves the business or becomes a problem. This can be addressed by good and bad leaver clauses to ensure that they can't just walk away with the shares when no longer adding value to the business.

See the link in Appendix 2 for the video on 'When to share a piece of the pie.'

How can I increase the value of my business?

With you and your leadership team focused on growing the business value, it is time to look at how that growth in value is achieved.

Here are some key areas to concentrate on.

Profitability and cash flow

As much as amazingly exciting forecasts look impressive, if you can show a potential purchaser or investor that you've already proven your potential by delivering some great historical results, they are much more likely to impact positively upon your valuation.

Strong gross and net profit margins, plus strong cash flow and working capital management are all important to demonstrate. Ensure your quotation system is accurate, your costs are well controlled and you have systems in place to ensure credit control over your debtors. Show that your assets are well managed and that there is a strategic plan for your renewals and new asset investments.

Taking a regular look at the business' own credit score will ensure that suppliers and potential customers feel comfortable working with you and will result in more cash flow for you.

Systemizing the business

By systemizing the business, you reduce the reliance on any individual and demonstrate that the business can operate independently of a single person – which is important for continuity if the founders are planning to exit the business.

To achieve a higher valuation, founders need to effectively make themselves redundant from the day-to-day operations of the business and ensure that others are responsible for selling the products and delivering the service.

While early stage businesses may struggle to cover the overheads for these additional costs, there are ways to mitigate the risk by using commission remuneration structures, especially for sales staff. The strategy should include the planned recruitment of a wider management and leadership team as soon as financially viable and the business owner can then begin to delegate to leverage the resources in the business and bring in processes to manage the growth.

Securing certainty for the future

If you can remove or mitigate the future risk within a business, investors or purchasers will feel more confident when predicting the financial projections of the company and their valuation will reflect that.

Aim to build recurring revenue streams with customers, have various routes to market and spread your sector exposure. Having predictable, even constant, costs if possible and a wide choice of suppliers will also ensure margins are able to be maintained.

And finally, the most important aspect will be to ensure your management information is reliable and you can measure your financial results on a timely basis. The ability to use these to predict future cash flows and profit trends is essential if you want to provide a potential investor or purchaser with sufficient comfort to value your business highly.

Increase your profile

Businesses with a known brand and strong reputation will be valued substantially higher than little-known businesses as they often attract competitive offers when the opportunity arises for an investor or a purchaser to capitalize on that profile.

Ensure that any overseas buyer or investor sees a positive view of your business online, considering all the possible points of exposure including third party content such as social media, press coverage and review sites.

Create intellectual property

The full value of a business includes the intangible, as well as the tangible financial assets in a company. These aren't always included in the business' Balance Sheet, so to support a higher valuation you should focus on being able to communicate this additional value to an investor or purchaser. The first step is to identify and document all your intellectual property and then protect it.

In addition, if any particular element of your intellectual property can directly support an income stream, and this is clear in your financial results, then this can be very persuasive to demonstrate your full value.

These steps rarely happen of their own accord and the most successful business owners have taken particular care to create a business that maximizes all these areas.

How do I sell my business?

Unless you have aspirations to be a serial entrepreneur, selling your company is usually a once in a lifetime experience, which can be quite intimidating unless you understand how the process usually works.

Whether we plan for it or not, one day we'll all have to exit our businesses. Will we sell to another company in our industry, some key members of staff as an MBO (Management Buy Out by the existing management team), an individual looking for an MBI (Management Buy-In by someone not currently working for the business), or we may even sell to our whole employee team. Every business situation and each deal is unique.

By choosing to plan our eventual exit, no matter how soon or far in the future it may be, you want to ensure that it becomes more valuable and more attractive to the greatest number of potential purchasers. After all, what are we building our businesses for?

Shouldn't we direct our efforts at building the most important and potentially most valuable asset we have – and then carving out our exit to recoup our efforts and investment? But before we get to that disposal process, maybe we'll choose to build our business first, to create more value for when we eventually choose to sell it.

Figure 5.2. Exit route map

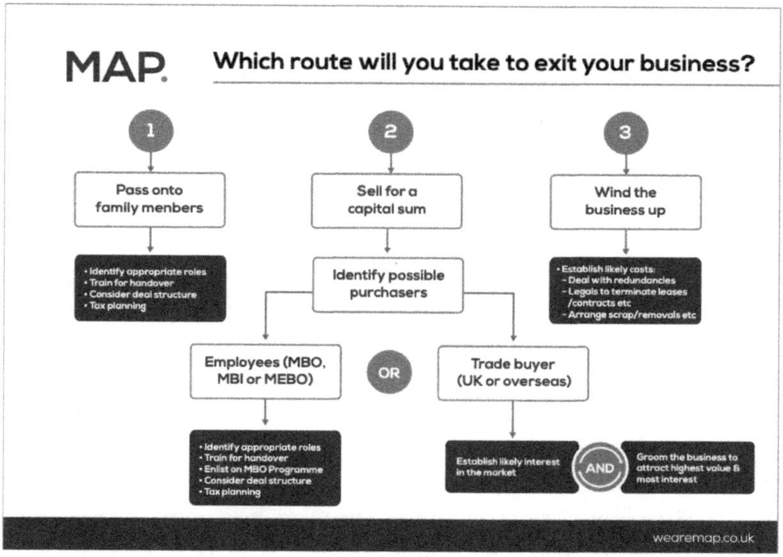

Source: MAP

The stages in a purchase or a sale are fairly standard and, irrespective of the size of the deal, follow a similar pattern each time. At MAP, we progress through the following steps.

Prepare your business for sale

Ideally, you will have been working towards a successful exit for years before you do actually decide to sell, as this will ensure you achieve the highest eventual valuation. Speak to us about our exit planning tools so you can focus on this as soon as possible.

Advertise the business for sale

While you can sometimes be approached by a potential purchaser, if you want to remain in control of this process, you will also want to encourage other competitive offers. You can't attract this interest unless you promote that your business is for sale, but to maintain confidentiality in the earliest stages, we would advise that we first send an anonymous flyer to the parties we consider to be the most likely potential purchasers. Those who are interested to investigate this opportunity will be asked to sign a confidentiality letter or non-disclosure agreement, after which we will share your business' name and then distribute more detailed information to them.

Open discussions with a view to reaching heads of terms

After sharing some information about your business, potential purchasers usually have some questions that they want to ask you in person and discuss the company in greater depth. We can attend these meetings to support you and they may also be accompanied by their corporate finance adviser or lawyer to these meetings. When we have narrowed down the most likely buyers, we will ask them to make an offer that contains the terms of the deal. When we have agreed which deal is most preferred, the potential purchaser will most likely ask for a period of exclusivity where we are not able to continue discussions with other parties to allow them time to conduct their due diligence.

Instruct lawyers to prepare documentation

When terms have been agreed then lawyers can be instructed to formalize the deal in the legal contracts. This is where warranties and indemnities are also discussed and agreed, where you provide some comfort for the purchaser, but your own exposure is also limited to the risk you are prepared to take. Other documents to be agreed may include ongoing consultancy or service agreements and property conveyancing or leases. Alongside these continuing negotiations, the purchaser will often be arranging their own funding if they require external finance in order to complete the deal, so many parties can become involved at this stage.

Completion

Immediately before completion, often only days or even hours before, the purchaser's lawyers will require some documents to verify the latest position and any items included in the warranties or indemnities. When the day of completion arrives, there are a multitude of documents to be signed, often electronically, and the lawyers will agree upon the timetable of how to manage this process. Following completion, there may be further work required by the parties' accountants; for example, there may be a requirement to prepare completion accounts to finalize what the eventual financial position of the company was on the day of the deal.

Managing this process can become quite time-consuming so we advise that you allow a corporate finance adviser to lead the transaction, allowing you to continue running your business effectively until the day that the deal is completed.

Figure 5.3. The business sale process

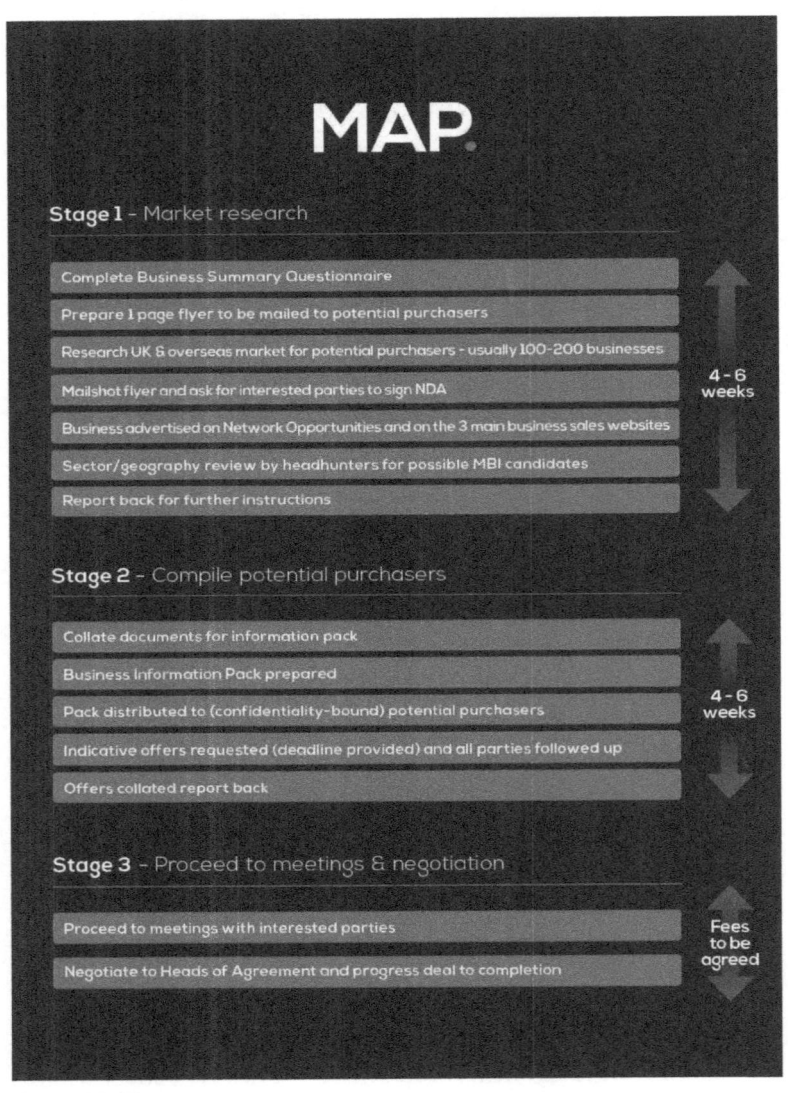

MAP.

Stage 1 - Market research

- Complete Business Summary Questionnaire
- Prepare 1 page flyer to be mailed to potential purchasers
- Research UK & overseas market for potential purchasers - usually 100-200 businesses
- Mailshot flyer and ask for interested parties to sign NDA
- Business advertised on Network Opportunities and on the 3 main business sales websites
- Sector/geography review by headhunters for possible MBI candidates
- Report back for further instructions

4-6 weeks

Stage 2 - Compile potential purchasers

- Collate documents for information pack
- Business Information Pack prepared
- Pack distributed to (confidentiality-bound) potential purchasers
- Indicative offers requested (deadline provided) and all parties followed up
- Offers collated report back

4-6 weeks

Stage 3 - Proceed to meetings & negotiation

- Proceed to meetings with interested parties
- Negotiate to Heads of Agreement and progress deal to completion

Fees to be agreed

Source: MAP

How do I buy a business?

A fast way to scale a business is by making strategic acquisitions. Either buying companies who are competitors or diversifying a little (such as vertical integration) or a lot (in a completely different sector). This allows businesses to scale much faster than by organic growth alone and can transform the size and direction of a company, almost overnight.

However, business owners should not enter into this lightly as it can be an expensive mistake if risks are not assessed and mitigated. Your strategy should be considered carefully.

Identifying suitable targets

Businesses are bought by purchasers for different reasons, maybe to increase market share and remove a competitor, to widen the scope of your reach to certain sectors or particular customers, or to acquire necessary skills or impressive intellectual property.

The most successful deals are those where synergies are obtained, which means that 1+1=3. Cost savings, especially from overheads, can help with the financial impact of an acquisition so that it makes sense mathematically. But far more impressive is when two businesses with different skill sets or ideas come together and the combination of this pairing brings creativity and results that neither could have achieved alone.

Start by identifying which types of businesses and which specific companies could provide this result for you. This begins by analyzing your existing business using a S.W.O.T. analysis, and in particular, focusing on how an acquisition could reduce the exposure you face from your current weaknesses or threats.

Using databases, you can then consider what size of business would be most appropriate, the location and likely value of the company, and begin to make anonymous approaches to business owners that fit these criteria.

How are deals funded?

On the whole, the most common form of finance in the market is actually vendor finance. Deferred consideration has been a staple of most SME acquisition deal structures for many years now and with the pressures on commercial funding due to the pandemic, this will continue to be the case. Acquisition loans may also be used as a very cost-effective option, since the lender has a valuable asset to secure against (the target company Balance Sheet) and it is important to look at all options when structuring a deal.

Agreeing a payment based on deferred consideration aids cash flow, but when the deal structure is also linked to earnouts dependent upon the level of the business' future results (i.e. turnover, profitability or retention of key customers or licences) then this means that shrewd purchasers can pick up a deal with little or no risk.

Mitigating risk

There are several parts of the process that aim to reduce the risk of buying a business. We've already discussed the first one, which is having a clear acquisition strategy.

Once you've identified a suitable business and an owner who is willing to enter into negotiations, the process rolls out and includes the following steps:

1. **Discussions with the business owner**: Do not underestimate your own 'gut feel' when meeting a business owner. If you are unsure as to the reality of what you are being told about the opportunity, be wary about progressing.
2. **The terms of the deal can be structured to mitigate risk**: For example, linking the price paid to certain conditions, which happen after completion (known as an earnout) or by retaining the vendor in a position where they are still responsible for carrying out certain tasks.
3. **Financial and commercial due diligence**: We assess the scope of this work according to the potential risks we are most concerned about, and we find evidence to assess those risks more meaningfully.

Extended: Mature financial thinking | 113

4. **Further due diligence or pre-contract enquiries**: The lawyers carry out further due diligence, or pre-contract enquiries, to measure the risk around other areas of the business.
5. **Warranties and indemnities**: These are included in the legal contracts as forms of promise or guarantees from the vendor. 'Disclosure' towards the end of the deal negotiations provides detailed evidence where the vendor cannot commit to certain clauses and then you can again assess whether you are willing to continue on the same basis.
6. **Integration**: While this occurs post-completion, it is essential that you have an integration plan that is developed ahead of time. This ensures that you maximize the opportunity brought by the acquisition and that practical issues don't interfere with the fulfilment of those expected synergies.

Figure 5.4. The acquisition strategy roadMAP

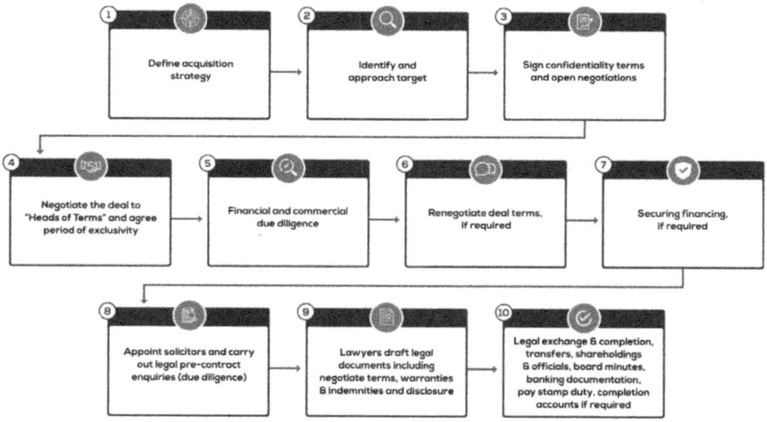

Source: MAP

The stages of an acquisition usually follow this process, irrespective of the size of the deal. Some stages are more fluid and may begin sooner than shown in Figure 5.4 (e.g. opening conversations with financiers) and several are carried out simultaneously (e.g.

legal due diligence and re-negotiating terms of the deal including warranties, etc).

This process can take weeks or months or sometimes even years! The key to success is to understand the reason for your acquisition and develop a strategy to identify and assess suitable target businesses.

A credible firm with experience in your sector will provide support throughout a deal and post-completion, so I recommend you open up these conversations early if you would like to explore a potential acquisition strategy in more detail.

Taking money and value out of your company

The most exciting tax planning that you can do is to work out how you can get more value out of the company for yourself!

There are up to 25 ways for a business owner to extract value from their business. All strategies should be considered collectively in order to maximize the value you take from the business in the most efficient way.

1: Salary

Generally, a salary should always be taken but kept to a low level. A minimal salary – above the lower earnings limit for national insurance contributions (NIC) – is important to retain access to state benefits such as the State Pension. The 'normal' basic salary depends on the business' overall employers' national insurance bill and the number of employees.

There are two scenarios:

i. A salary of around the primary threshold for NIC is usually the norm where there are multiple employees and there is enough of the employers' national insurance 'employment allowance' available. There should be no NICs payable in this scenario.

ii. If there is only one employee of the company or if the employers' national insurance 'employment allowance' is already used or not available, the norm is usually the secondary threshold for NIC, again to ensure no national insurance is payable.

There are lots of exceptions to the norm that can make taking a higher salary more suitable, such as:

- Where you can't take dividends or have an agreed or fixed amount of value to take out of the business (e.g. directors in investor backed businesses).
- If you are heavily involved in 'research and development' your salary can qualify for enhanced relief against corporation tax, which makes it more efficient to pay a higher salary (as opposed to dividends).
- The 'employment allowance' (an allowance against employers' national insurance, provided the total secondary class 1 NIC liabilities are below £100,000 in the previous tax year) can mean a higher salary can be paid without incurring employers' national insurance contributions; for example, this could make it worthwhile to have a salary around the value of the personal allowance – here the only cost would be the employee national insurance.
- An employee who is over State Pension age will not pay NICs. So, for example, a 68-year-old could have a salary at the value of the personal allowance with no tax or NIC (if the employment allowance is available).
- If you are looking for a mortgage or to re-mortgage (or other personal loan), some lenders will base their credit scoring on employment income (rather than dividends).

2: Employing your spouse or family members

If they have a lower overall income than you, consider employing a spouse/civil partner or family member so that the company can benefit from the additional resource; the individual can use their personal allowances and/or lower level tax bands, and the company can make a national insurance saving.

It is important that their pay can be justified in terms of actual activities on behalf of the company. For a single employee company, employing an additional employee may also make the employment allowance available.

3: Dividends

After salary, the most commonly used method to take the remaining amount of desired cash from the company is via dividends. Dividends to the value of the dividend allowance are tax free, so where possible this amount should be taken as a dividend annually.

Dividend values in excess of the dividend allowance and taxable income threshold for the basic rate income tax band, the tax rate on dividends is relatively low at the current rate of 8.75%, but for values in excess of this, the method of taking value becomes much more important. When your total income goes above the taxable income threshold for the basic rate income tax band, you pay a higher rate of tax, for example 33.75% on dividends.[2] You could also lose entitlement to certain benefits and allowances; for example, child benefit, tax-free savings allowance is reduced.

Sometimes you may want to take a large amount out of the business; for example, for a large purchase. One option could be to vote a dividend. The highest tax rate on dividends is 39.35% (once total income is taxed at the additional rate income tax rate),

---

[2] *Rate as at 2024.*

which, while lower than the tax rate on a salary or bonus, is still relatively high.[3]

So, before voting a dividend, alternative tax planning options, of which there are many, should be considered with a tax specialist. For example, if a business owner wants to extract funds to invest in property, buy a car, give money to family or start a new business venture, there may be better ways to structure it from a goal, commercial and tax perspective.

Examples of options in this regard are (a) larger pension contributions (e.g. to fund a commercial property acquisition), and (b) family investment companies where the income and gains from the investments can be spread among family members.

4: Giving shares to family members

If you receive dividends from the company, you should consider giving some shares to your spouse/civil partner if they pay tax at a lower rate than you. This means they will be able to use the dividend tax-free allowance, and any other lower rate bands than yours.

Away from your spouse, you could also give shares to children (over 18) or other family members, but the capital gains tax position would need to be considered before doing this.

5: Pensions

Making company contributions to the business owner's private or company pension scheme can be a tax efficient way to extract further value from a business. However, certain annual limits apply to cap contribution levels.

---

[3] *Rate as at 2024.*

Registered pension schemes

It's important to consider the lifestyle that you want when you stop running your business. What level of comfort do you require? What value of assets do you need to accumulate and what level of income do you want? These are important questions that deserve consideration as part of an overall strategy. Carrying out a full individual and corporate tax diagnostic is essential to ensure these issues are considered as a collective; for example, building the value of your business, building your personal wealth and structuring all your affairs with long-term goals in mind.

Here, we are only focusing on pensions through the lens of maximizing value that you can extract from your business. Once you have established the amount you can extract from the business using the methods detailed above, you should then identify a surplus that can be used towards retirement provision.

Pensions can be a very tax efficient way to put money aside as you pay no income tax or national insurance when the money is paid in (subject to the limits detailed below). You also get a corporation tax deduction on the money paid in.

Income or capital gains generated from funds or assets within the pension are not taxed. The fund can be accessed tax efficiently from age 55. On withdrawal, a lump sum of up to 25% of the fund can be accessed tax free.[4] Withdrawal of the remainder is taxed but can be spread across multiple tax years, making the most of the personal allowances and tax rates.

How much can be paid in?

The maximum annual amount that can be contributed – with no income tax or national insurance, but a full corporation tax deduction – is known as the annual allowance. The annual

---

[4] *Rate as at 2024.*

allowance applies across all pension schemes; it is not a 'per scheme' allowance. If you earn over the adjusted income figure for the annual allowance, you are likely to have a restricted annual allowance. The allowance is reduced by £1 for every £2 in annual earnings above this figure, subject to a minimum allowance.

Where this maximum is unused in a particular tax year, the balance may be carried forward by up to three years and added to the annual allowance for the relevant year. As an example, if you have not previously contributed, the business could put up to £180,000 as a one-off contribution, receiving a full corporation tax deduction and with no income tax or national insurance.

The amount you can pay in is not limited to what you earn; for example, even if your salary is £8,840, the business could put anything up to the annual allowance into your pension, or even more if the 'carry forward' option is available. This is provided you were a member of a registered pension scheme in those previous years and based on current allowances. If you contribute to your pension personally from your gross pay, your tax relief is limited to how much you earned that particular year.

If you contribute in excess of your annual allowance or accumulated annual allowances if you are carrying them forward, you will trigger a tax charge called the annual allowance charge. It is added to your taxable income and taxed at your rate of tax (basic, higher or additional rate). It is effectively reclaiming the tax benefit incurred on the excess contribution. If the charge is over £2,000, you can speak to your pension provider to see if the pension can pay the charge from the fund. The company, on the other hand, is not subject to any penalties and can still claim a corporation tax deduction on the full amount.

6: Loans

There are various scenarios to consider when it comes to loans – from money already lent to the company to having money available to loan to the company. Making loans to the company can be a tax efficient investment where a commercial rate of interest can be paid to the business owner. Employee loans under £10,000 can be an effective way to motivate and retain key members of the team.

Loaning money to the business and employee loans

You may have historically lent money to the company or have funds available to lend to the company. Or alternatively the company may have money it can lend to you or the employees. Each of these scenarios is considered below.

Scenario one: You have already lent money to the company

In this instance, generally the company should be paying you interest because:

- It makes commercial and legal sense to protect your investment.
- The income will be 'savings income', which, if you haven't used your savings allowance, you can receive up to the personal savings allowance tax free per year.

In many instances, business owners have lent money to the company in years gone by and don't realize that the loan can be taken back out of the company tax free at a future point. This is important to remember, as it can form part of your value extraction strategy once funds are available in the company to repay your loan with no tax consequences.

Scenario two: You have funds available to lend to the company

Before deciding whether to lend to the company, you need to also consider the commercial risk factors and seek independent financial advice, for example, if you make an unsecured loan, the funds are available to the company and could be used to pay other creditors in the event of trading difficulties. Generally speaking, if you have savings as cash, it will be earning very little interest.

So it can make sense to instead lend some money to the company because:

- The company will benefit from the additional cash flow.
- The interest you receive will be tax free up to your 'personal savings allowance'. In a lot of circumstances, the tax saving made will exceed the total amount of interest you would have earned by investing the money elsewhere.

The specific tax savings depends on your overall position, but at worst it represents the ability to get an additional amount from the company tax free.

Other considerations and planning points

Where payments of interest represent 'yearly interest', there is a requirement for the company to withhold 20% of each interest payment and pay it to HMRC (via a quarterly CT61 return). This can increase the administrative burden. If interest payments are not 'yearly interest' then generally withholding tax does not apply. An example of loan interest that is not 'yearly interest' is where the loan term does not exceed 12 months.

The rate of interest charged has to be commercially justifiable (e.g. by reference to an unsecured loan from a third party) and generally can be anywhere between 5% and 15%.

It is very important to properly document the arrangement to reduce risk of any future dispute, whether with the company or HMRC. Provided the terms are legally documented, this often represents a low-risk method of extracting funds from the company tax efficiently.

Scenario three: The company has funds to lend to you or your employees

If the company has spare cash flow, it can be a good way to incentivize you and your employees by offering up to £10,000 loans, interest free. This provides a good benefit as the employee can invest the funds or help them with cash flow to purchase something. It can also act as a good retention tool as employees will have to repay the loan if they leave.

7: *Business assets*

Business owners who allow their company to use personal assets should consider charging rent for the use. This is another effective way to extract funds from a business tax free. Certain business owned assets can be used by a business owner without any tax implications provided private use is minimal.

Rent

The company may be using assets that are owned by directors/shareholder, or those individuals are considering acquiring a property to be rented to the company.

This can be commercially attractive in some circumstances, examples of which are:

- Asset protection – keeping the building and fixtures and fittings out of company ownership.
- Your pension is maxed out either annually or lifetime allowance.
- You don't want to commit to large pension contributions in the short term.
- You are looking to buy a property personally and then rent to the company, and due to other factors (e.g. shareholding structure or lack of funds available in the company) it makes sense to buy the property personally.
- Assets already in ownership, for example, commercial building or other assets, and you don't want to transfer them to the company for commercial or tax reasons.

It can also be tax efficient to hold the asset personally and rent it to the company.

Example in the scenario where dividends are not possible
Consider someone with a £50,000 salary, who owns a property personally that is used by the company. The market value rent for the property is around £22,800.

- If the company paid £20,000 as a salary or a bonus, it would cost £22,760 (£20,000 plus employers' NIC) with a tax and NIC cost of £11,160.[5]
- If £22,760 was paid as rent, the tax cost would be £9,104.[6]

In this example, the saving in comparison to salary is nearly £2,056.

If you sell the asset alongside the shares in the business at a future date, you would usually be able to claim business asset disposal relief to reduce the tax you pay to 10% of the gain.

Unfortunately, the payment of rent by the company can restrict the relief available when you sell the asset. The relief is restricted by the percentage of market rent paid by the company. So, if the business pays full market rent, no relief is available.

Furthermore, business property relief can be restricted, increasing potential exposure to inheritance tax. As the asset is owned by you, it will be in your estate when you pass away. Business assets owned by you personally only receive 50% relief, so the remainder is currently taxed at 40% (known as the standard inheritance tax rate) if your estate exceeds the inheritance tax nil rate band.

For both reliefs, specialist advice should be taken to ensure relief is maximized.

---

[5] *For income tax and NICs at current 2024 rates, see www.gov.uk/government/publications/rates-and-allowances-national-insurance-contributions/rates-and-allowances-national-insurance-contributions*

[6] *For income tax but no NICs at current 2024 rates, see www.gov.uk/government/publications/rates-and-allowances-national-insurance-contributions/rates-and-allowances-national-insurance-contributions*

Personal use of company assets

If you are considering purchasing an asset that will have a business use, you should consider if you can pay for it via the company as an effective way to maximize the value you take out of your business. Where appropriate, the savings could include income tax, NIC, corporation tax and VAT.

While a tablet/ iPad has the capability to make video and voice calls, it cannot be treated as a mobile phone and falls into the mobile phone exemption. The asset must be bought and used primarily for business purposes. It will be taxable on you if there is significant personal use, little or no requirement for you to have an asset for your work or it is a reward for your employment. In some cases, the personal use of the asset may be exempt despite the personal use exceeding the business use. This would only apply if the private use is secondary to the use for work purposes.

Example of company assets
If your role requires you to use a laptop for most of the day, it will not be taxable if you use the laptop for personal use during the evenings or weekend. Clearly, your personal use would be insignificant to the business use. Compare this to an individual who works in a trade like manufacturing and only needs a laptop for invoicing and time sheets but has some personal use of the laptop.

HMRC will allow personal use of the laptop provided you need the laptop to carry out the duties of the employment even if the amount of time spent on private use exceeds the business use. The laptop must be sufficient to carry out the invoicing and time sheets. You wouldn't be able to buy an expensive laptop that you want to use for your film editing hobby and claim it was for business purposes as you wouldn't need that spec of laptop to carry out your business duties.

8: Employee benefits

Normally, if a benefit is provided to you, it will be taxed in the same way as a salary. However, there are some exceptions to this rule (detailed below) that can result in significant cost savings, in the form of corporation tax, VAT, income tax and NIC.

For example, if a cost can be incurred by the business, the equivalent saving (ignoring VAT savings) on the monthly cost could be:

- 25% if you take dividends and are a basic rate taxpayer.
- 45% if you take dividends and are a higher rate taxpayer.
- 40% if you are salaried and are a basic rate taxpayer.
- 49% if you are salaried and are a higher rate taxpayer.

Given the saving, consideration should be given to the following costs and whether they can be purchased by the business rather than personally.

9: Life insurance

Relevant life assurance (sometimes referred to as a relevant life policy) is similar to a life insurance policy that a director or employee may have in their personal names. The policy is owned by and premiums are paid by the employer.

If you set up a relevant life assurance policy, it is a tax-free (income tax and NIC) benefit for the individuals involved. There will also be no NIC cost for you as the employer.

The cost of the policy can be treated as a deductible expense and reduce the company's corporation tax bill provided certain conditions are met.

10: Pensions advice

If you need to seek pensions advice, it is tax free up to £500 in value if it is paid for by the business provided certain conditions apply such as availability to employees, or age or ill health of employees.

11: Mobile phones

One mobile phone can be given to every employee in the business – including you and any family members that are employed – and there is no tax or NIC regardless of whether the phone is used for personal calls, messaging, etc. It may also be attractive to employees to have a phone that is better than one they would otherwise have if they bought a phone personally.

It is also possible for the company to offer a second mobile phone to you and certain employees provided the phone has insignificant personal usage. In other words, the main reason for providing the second phone to you is for business purposes. This would allow employees who want separation of home and work matters to have two mobile phones.

A tablet that allows you access to make calls via Skype or FaceTime isn't deemed to be a mobile phone – it is treated as an employee use of a business asset.

12: Anything except cash that costs less than £50

This is subject to specific restrictions detailed below, but in short you could buy anything via the business as a way to extract value, for example, your favourite bottle of perfume/ aftershave, an Amazon gift card to buy something for your house or take your family for a meal while on holiday, provided it costs less than £50 (known as trivial benefits). This is an effective way to extract value from your business.

For you as a director, the total amount that can be spent per year on items like this is £300. For other employees, the amount is uncapped.

You can be given up to £300 in 'gifts' annually, provided certain conditions are met:

i. Each gift value must not exceed £50.
ii. Each gift must not be cash or something that can be turned into cash. This means things like Amazon vouchers or supermarket vouchers are fine, provided they can't be traded in for cash.
iii. It must not be part of their contract or salary.
iv. It must not be in recognition of services (i.e. performance related).

If family members are employed by the company, they can also be given up to £300 in gifts in the same way. If family members who are not employed are given gifts, this counts towards the director's £300 cap.

For other employees, the gift amount is uncapped. Giving benefits like this to staff can be massively rewarding for them, helping to achieve motivated staff and high retention levels.

13: Staff functions

Provided the cost per attendee is less than £150, an event for staff, for example at Christmas, is not taxable on you or your employees. As an example, a business with five employees could each take a guest to an event. Provided the total cost is less than £1,500, it falls within the exemption detailed above.

This exemption can be aggregated over the year, so, for example, you could have two events costing £75 per head and it would still be tax free.

14: Employee car parking

Paying for a car parking space for yourself or an employee can be very beneficial for city centre businesses where the cost of parking can be high. The car park space must be at or near to your office to be tax free. VAT registered businesses can also reclaim the VAT element of the cost, giving a further saving. This can also be a very efficient way to reward employees who need to drive to a place of work and have to park in an expensive car park.

15: Training

Work training can cover a wide range of areas that are wholly for business purposes, such as professional development and health and safety. Instead of incurring the cost personally, the business can pay for your training as a tax-free benefit.

16: Other tax efficient benefits

Outside of the 'tax-free' benefits listed above, other benefits that can be provided by a company to you and your employees in a tax efficient way are detailed in the next four sections.

Lunches and snacks

Provided all staff are offered the option, providing lunches to staff at the business premises is tax free for the employees, and the business can claim corporation tax relief and recover VAT (where relevant) on the costs. The conditions to qualify are that the lunches must be available to all employees, be 'reasonable' and provided at the business premises (e.g. canteen or kitchen area).

Childcare support

There are two potential ways to help fund childcare in a tax efficient way:

i. Tax-free childcare is a scheme that allows you to save up to 20% on childcare costs. The government will contribute a certain amount per tax year.

ii. Workplace creches – while not practical for most businesses, a workplace creche can be provided to you and your employees with no tax or national insurance liability. So, if applicable, it is worth considering further.

Bicycles and equipment cycle to work

Bicycles and equipment can be purchased under a 'salary sacrifice' scheme so that the cost of the bike and equipment comes out of pay before being taxed; it offers equivalent savings to the 'tax-free' benefits listed above. This has a tax and national insurance saving for the individual and also gives a national insurance saving to the company. This saving can also be passed on to you to make it even cheaper to get the bike (and equipment).

The amount that can be spent is now uncapped. So a top quality bike and equipment (helmet, gear, lights, etc) can be bought with significant savings available.

The way the schemes work in practice is that there is an initial rental period (usually 12–24 months) after which you can hand the bike back, buy it at its current value, or continue to rent it from the cycle scheme provider at low cost. Choosing the last option is usually the most cost effective, meaning you can own the bike outright after four or so years.

An example of a cycle scheme provider and videos on how it works can be found in Appendix 2.

Onsite gyms and sorting facilities

As a way to promote the health and wellbeing of you and your staff, you can offer access to sports or recreational facilities, or non-cash vouchers that can only be used to access those facilities as a benefit.

There is an exemption from tax if:

- The facilities are available to all employees.
- It is not open to members of the general public.
- The facilities are used wholly or mainly by employees, former employees or family members of those groups.

If multiple businesses use one set of facilities, this does not trigger a benefit. This would apply to office gyms, shared gyms in communal office space and recreational facilities.

17: Taxable benefits still worth considering

It is also worth considering other benefits that can be offered to you and your employees. While not 'tax free' or available as a 'salary sacrifice' scheme, they can have other benefits, such as:

i. You may get better rates or premiums for bulk buying for a number of individuals. Specific examples of the types of products worth considering are:
   - Medical cover: this definitely meets all the benefits listed above.
   - Many policies have discounted gym memberships, offers and promotions for mental and physical wellbeing.
   - Some policies allow members to reclaim dentistry and optician costs. This can be hugely beneficial for you and your employees and in some cases may outweigh the tax cost of having the benefit.
   - It is worth noting that medical insurance policies that cover only injuries or diseases that result from your work are tax free.
   - If your medical insurance doesn't cover this, your business can pay for your medical treatment when you are working overseas.

ii. Increased wellbeing and productivity of staff.

iii. Better quality products and rewards than employees would otherwise get if they had their own policy or didn't have a policy at all.
iv. It's just a good employee perk!
- Policies can give quicker and no-cost access to care in the event of illness or injury. Again, this can be very valuable in giving you and your employees top quality support in times of need.
- Shareholder protection insurance. This type of policy will allow things like remaining shareholders to buy out the family of a deceased shareholder.
- Critical illness cover or income protection insurance. Again, while taxable on you and your employees, it can be hugely incentivizing for employees to have things like this covered by the company.

18: Company cars

Where company cars are provided for specific individuals, a taxable benefit will arise on the employee. This is based on a percentage of the list price of the vehicle, determined by its CO_2 emissions. The use of lower emissions vehicles can generate significant tax savings.

Example of a company car

As an example, consider a company car valued at £35,000 for a higher rate taxpayer:

i. High emissions cars attract a benefit in kind (BIK) of up to 37% of the list price; BIK of £12,950, at a cost of £5,180 for the employee (and £1,787 for the employer).
ii. Low emissions cars attract a BIK of between 2% and 14% depending on when registered, the CO_2 output and the

electric-only driving range; for a 14% car, BIK of £4,900, at a cost of £1,960 for the employee (and £676 for the employer).

iii. Zero emissions cars (i.e. fully electric cars or plug in hybrids if they have an electric-only range of more than 130 miles) attract a BIK of 2%; BIK of £700, at a cost of £280 for the employee (and £97 for the employer). The rate will increase up to 5% between April 2025 and April 2028.

In this example the employee saves £3,220 every year just by choosing a lower emissions vehicle, and the employer saves £1,111. If the employee chooses a zero emissions vehicle, the saving to the employee versus a high emissions car is £4,900, and the employer saves £1,690.

Fuel costs provided by the company will be subject to an additional BIK charge unless the cost of fuel is in relation to journeys that are part of the employee's business duties, for example, a service engineer travelling to an appointment.

When a company car is purchased, you cannot recover VAT on the purchase unless it will be used exclusively for business purposes and not made available for private use. If you lease a car, you can recover 50% of the VAT (the 50% block is to cover private use).

Electric cars

An electric car can mean a 'pure-electric' car or a 'hybrid' (part petrol/diesel and part electric). The key tax advantage available if the car meets the relevant conditions is low tax on the individual user.

There is no difference in the VAT recovery on purchases and leases of electric cars compared to hybrid or standard fuel cars despite it being an environmentally friendly vehicle.

Charging for electric vehicles

The cost of charging electric vehicles at the place of employment is exempt from tax and NICs. It makes no difference who owns the car. It is also possible for you to receive a tax-free benefit if a charging point is installed at your home provided you have a company car. It would be taxable if you had a charging point installed at home to charge your personal car that you used for business purposes.

Running costs for company owned cars

With the exception of fuel (which will result in an additional BIK charge for non-business use), the BIK charge covers all motor running costs, including costs such as servicing and insurance.

Where a vehicle is currently provided, but insurance is not, the company should consider providing insurance too – the increased cost will be deductible for corporation tax purposes, but no additional tax charge will arise on you.

Additional items for company owned cars

Ordinarily, car accessories are included in the value of the vehicle when calculating the company car tax charge. However, there are two company car accessories you could purchase via your business that are completely tax free:

i. Personalized number plates.
ii. Hands free kits and equipment – if you need a cradle for your mobile phone or a cable to charge your phone, it is possible to purchase them via your business.

19: Business expenses paid for personally

Expenses of the business that have been paid for personally may either be reimbursed by the company or, if not reimbursed, may be deductible for the individual against other income. You can put any cost through your business, but it doesn't mean that it is tax free.

The rules can be complex with grey areas, so care needs to be taken to ensure you claim properly. Where an employee incurs expenses in the course of their employment:

- For the company, any cost incurred in reimbursing expenses will be deductible against corporation tax.
- For the employee, the position is often more complex, as explained below.

Non-taxable

Where you incur expenses 'wholly, exclusively and necessarily' for the purpose of your employment, amounts received will be free from tax or NICs. Similarly, if the expense is not reimbursed, a tax and NIC refund can often be claimed (usually via self-assessment).

The rules on relief can be restrictive. In particular, where expenses are partly for another job, or for personal reasons, relief may not be available. While there may be grey areas, there are certain types of personal expenditure – such as uniforms, protective clothing or business mileage – that can almost always be successfully claimed.

Taxable

If the expense is not 'wholly, exclusively and necessarily' for the purpose of your employment, any reimbursement will give rise to income tax and NIC implications, as an employment benefit.

The specific tax implications will depend on a variety of factors, including whether the expense relates to travel and subsistence (including mileage allowance), home working expenses, whether the expense is reimbursed or a bill is instead paid on your behalf, to name a few.

These costs could be added to your director's loan account to stop the benefit being taxable. However, you would need to repay

Extended: Mature financial thinking | 135

this balance within nine months of the company's accounting period to avoid a 32.5% tax charge (albeit reimbursable if you put the money back into the company later).

Read the next five sections for guidance on business expenses paid for personally:

20: Home working expenses

The rules around working from home allowances has changed since April 2022 given the change in COVID restrictions. Working from home allowances are typically only relevant to fully remote businesses now and perhaps some other businesses with specific arrangements.

If one or more of the below conditions apply, your business can give £6 per week or £26 per month for home working as a tax-free perk:

- The business doesn't have an office.
- There are no appropriate facilities available for the employee to perform their job on their employer's premises.
- The employee's job requires them to live far away from the office.

If the cost of working from home is greater than £6 a week (£26 a month), we recommend that detailed records are kept as evidence; itemized billing for the extra cost of heating and lighting to back up the amount being paid to staff. The amount must be fair and reasonable such as considering usage, the proportion in terms of the areas of the home and how long it is used for work purposes compared to other use.

Your client cannot reimburse items that have a dual purpose such as council tax, rent, water rates, etc. Where this is done, again there should be no income tax or NICs on the additional payments.

Here's an example of how this calculation works:

> Director one has a three-bedroom home with eight rooms in total. One of the rooms is used for eight hours per day, five days per week as an office. The gas and electricity bill is £5,000 per year.
>
> You'd divide £5,000 over the number of rooms = £625.
>
> A full time worker has roughly 230 workdays per year (you should use an online tool to work out the workdays for the actual year and deduct their holiday allowance from this). Then, you'd divide £625 by 365 and multiply by 230 = £293.
>
> If the room is used by the family for a few hours an evening to watch TV or as a bedroom, you'd need to pro-rate this further.

In this example, it would be better to claim the HMRC's exempt amount of £26 per month given it is £312 per year compared to £293 for usage.

If a broadband connection is needed in order for the employee to work from home, and one is not already available, the provision of the connection can be paid for by the company and not result in a taxable benefit. However, any private use must be limited. In reality, this will rarely apply as most homes have a broadband connection these days.

21: Mileage claims

Where you use your own car for business (excluding commuting to and from work), you can currently claim 45p for each business mile travelled up to 10,000 miles and 25p per mile thereafter, without income tax consequences. These are known as HMRC approved mileage rates.

An additional optional 5p per mile can be paid where you have 'car pooled' with a fellow employee or director. Similarly, for motorcycles 24p per mile can be paid, and for bicycles 20p per mile can be paid, tax free. The company can also claim a tax deduction for mileage payments paid to employees.

Congestion charge – company car

If you incur the congestion charge while travelling to London using your company car, you can put the cost of the charge through the business.

22: Business travel

Travelling to and from 'the office'

Ordinarily, you are unable to put the costs of commuting to and from the office through the business. This applies to the cost of petrol or public transport, as well as claiming back 45p per mile as detailed above. So, can I claim for the costs of going to the office if I usually work from home or only go to the office on an infrequent basis?

Your business address is deemed to be your 'office'. It is your main place of business that you regularly or usually attend even if it is infrequently. If you choose to work at home and do not go into the office very often, this doesn't change the fact that you are commuting to your workplace when you do go into the office (provided that is the place you usually attend for all of your employment). There are some exceptions to this that you should be aware of.

Late night working costs
If you need to get a taxi home from the office as you have been working late (until at least 9pm), you can get the business to pay for the taxi to get home without any tax implications. This must be irregular; you are required to work late for a business

reason and where the public transport has stopped or it would be unreasonable to use it. This can be used up to 60 journeys per year and has no maximum amount per journey.

Failed car share arrangement
This also applies if car sharing arrangements fail after you have arrived at work due to unforeseen circumstances. For example, if your lift home with another director or employee isn't possible as they have had to go home due to illness, this would also apply.

Public travel costs
You can claim for the cost of public transport costs if travelling for business such as client meetings or to attend an industry conference.

Private travel versus public transport
As outlined above, you can claim for the private usage of your personal car if you travel for business. It is a commercial decision as to whether you travel in your car or take public transport. Usually this will be considered based on cost, location, travel time, equipment taken and time of day.

As an example, it may be cheaper to take the train to Birmingham but it is necessary to take the car instead as you are required to take some equipment with you and the combined cost of public transport and courier costs is more than the cost of claiming mileage back.

Another example may be that the location of the business meeting is in the middle of the countryside so public transport will be ruled out.

First-class travel versus standard class travel
Generally, the cost of the business travel will not normally have any bearing on whether or not tax relief can be claimed. A claim for business class travel over standard class wouldn't be denied if it was necessary for the journey.

Here are some examples where first/business class travel is necessary:

- You were travelling with a client who is booked on first/business class travel.
- You are travelling on a long journey, so you need more space for comfort – say to sleep while on the journey ahead of a meeting when you arrive at your destination.
- You require privacy and space to carry out your work while using public transport – say you require a desk for your laptop and place for your files while working, which is only possible in first class.

Airport lounges
Following the above points, an airport lounge could be claimed as a business expense if required for commercial purposes. An example could be that you need space and privacy to carry out your work while waiting for your flight.

Taxi versus public transport
You could also claim for the cost of a taxi if you were unable to take public transport. This may be due to speed, time of the day, location or equipment taken. There must be a commercial reason for claiming the taxi over public transport to claim the cost back.

For example, you couldn't claim the cost of taking a taxi for a 10-mile journey during the day where you could easily take a train instead and had no reason to take the taxi apart from the fact you prefer not to use a train.

However, you could claim a taxi to your hotel when arriving in London if you had a large suitcase containing clothing for a week of business meetings as it would be unsafe and impractical to use the tube.

Personal element
If your travel involves any personal element, it is still eligible if the purpose of the travel is for business and does not involve a detour. For example, you travel to London for the day for a work conference and meet a friend for a coffee before you head home. You can still claim the cost of the train travel provided the reason to travel to London is for business.

Another example could be that you travel to London for a work conference on a Friday and decide to stay in London over the weekend as a holiday. You book your train ticket back home for the Sunday evening when your break ends. It would be possible to claim the cost of this travel as business provided the main reason for going to London was for the work conference. You wouldn't be able to claim any expenses for food or accommodation after the event finished.

Travel to a temporary workplace
You are unable to claim back the costs of commuting to your office. However, you can claim for travel to a workplace that you don't go to regularly or for short periods of time.

An example may be that you are required to work at head office for occasional meetings or you need to work at another new office for a set period of time to get the office up and running.

If you are responsible for an area over which you perform duties, then the travel expenses for covering that area are allowable such as a regional director travelling to different business premises. The travel to various sites does not constitute ordinary commuting as none of the locations would be considered permanent places of work.

23: Subsistence and entertaining

If you are carrying out your director duties, such as attending a client meeting or travelling for business, you can claim your meals and drinks back via expenses tax free provided receipts are retained.

Say you are attending a client meeting, you could claim back your lunch while in the city centre or claim back a coffee on your way to a supplier meeting. Another example is you might buy your evening meal at a service station on your way back from a client meeting as it will be too late to eat when you arrive home.

Incidental overnight expenditure

If you are travelling on business and are required to stay overnight, you can claim £5 in the UK or £10 overseas per night for incidental travel costs without any receipts.

As an example, this may be a newspaper, refreshments from the mini bar, laundry, home phone calls, tip for a taxi driver or porter. The limits must include VAT paid. If you exceed this limit per night, the whole amount becomes taxable as employment income rather than the excess over £5 or £10.

If you are away for an unbroken run of consecutive nights, you do not need to necessarily claim £5 per night. HMRC compare the total of the exemptions for each night against the total payment. Say you spend £25 on a five-night business trip. One night you spent £7, one night you spent £3 and the other nights you spend £5, this would be allowable as it doesn't exceed £25, which it is the total limit for five nights away.

Entertaining

When you are entertaining a client, your business can cover the cost of entertaining provided it is reasonable and for business purposes. This may include lunch or dinner, drinks including alcohol or attendance at a sporting event such as a football or tennis match. This may be to thank them for their business, to discuss a new deal or to promote a better working relationship.

You can also use this as a way of extracting value personally from the business. You could take a customer to a restaurant you have always wanted to try or a sporting event for your favourite football team.

Unfortunately, the company is unable to claim client entertaining as an expense against their profits and no VAT can be reclaimed for these costs.

You may be considering paying for a corporate box at a football stadium or the like. The treatment of them is different depending on how you use them and who uses them. If you take a client to the corporate box, the normal rules apply so the cost cannot be deducted from your business profits and no VAT can be recoverable. However, it wouldn't be a taxable benefit for you as a director as you are entertaining a client as part of your duties.

You could also consider taking a group of employees to the box to entertain a group of clients as this would be tax free provided it is required as part of their employment duties. If you used the box to entertain your staff or you went to the box with a group of friends, it would be a taxable benefit on you and your employees. Income tax and national insurance would be payable on the benefit.

Music, audio books and Amazon Prime subscriptions

If you are currently paying for a music, audio book or Amazon Prime subscription, you should consider putting the cost of these subscriptions through the business.

HMRC will only allow the business to claim a corporation tax deduction for these costs if they are only used for business purposes. It would also be tax free for you and your employees. A key point to note is that you will be required to register for a music licence if you are playing music in your office even if it is on headphones.

Examples of music, audio books and Amazon Prime subscriptions

You have a subscription to Audible that you use only to listen to books about your industry and books which cover business strategy, planning and other related content. You could claim this cost from the business.

You have a Spotify licence that you use to play music in the office and when staff are working from home. Your team have put together playlists that reflect the business values. They listen to them at home and in the office to remind them of the business values and create unity. You could also claim this cost from the business.

You have an Amazon Prime account which you use to buy items for the business such as computer equipment, stationery, etc. You could also claim this cost from the business.

24: Points rewards cards

If you or an employee has a personal card that you use for business expenses, any points received from the reward card are not taxable on you. A good example of this is air miles cards where significant air miles can be accumulated – leading to big discounts on flights.

Similarly, a company card that receives points (such as air miles) can be used by the business owner to accumulate points and pay for flights without any tax or NIC on the individual. For an example of this type of rewards card, please see the American Express link in Appendix 2.

25: Education fees planning

When funding private education, you will expend significant amounts of income for the benefit of another individual, after it has been taxed on you.

Where the income is instead taxable on those in education, this can make the payment of education fees more tax efficient. Substantial tax savings can arise, due to the personal allowance and basic rate band, which are typically unused by children in education.

However, where the beneficiaries are minors the gift must not be made by the parents, as it would be rendered ineffective for tax purposes under the 'parental settlement rules'. Instead, the settlement should be made by grandparents/other family members.

Tax planning

Suitable relatives will not always own income producing assets themselves. However, if they have sufficient wealth they could acquire suitable assets, such as property or shares.

Advice must be sought to ensure that any tax planning undertaken is not caught by HMRC's anti-avoidance rules given the risks involved. As an example, tax planning that seeks to avoid tax or reduce tax by allowing the directors, who are also the main shareholders (the owners) of a company, to divert dividend income from themselves to their minor children via close family members such as grandparents or aunties/uncles is ineffective and caught by anti-avoidance.

Care must be taken where there is parental involvement. In particular, reciprocal agreements between the parents and other family members must be avoided.

Educational trusts

Although gifts can often be made to the children outright, it is usually preferable to gift assets into a trust for educational purposes. This route would allow you to retain control as trustee (or via a letter of wishes), while the income tax advantages would still be available in the correct circumstances.

Bespoke advice should be sought on the best option.

Research and development

I couldn't finish this section on tax planning without mentioning research and development (R&D). The SME R&D scheme (research and development tax credit for small- and medium-sized enterprises) was introduced in 2000.

It allows companies to reduce their corporation tax liabilities based on their enhanced R&D expenditure or to claim a payable tax credit if the company is loss making.

The relief rates and terms have changed several times since the scheme was first introduced, but it remains a well-used and very attractive opportunity for many digital agencies.

The work that your company carries out that qualifies for R&D tax relief must be part of a specific project to make an advance in science or technology. To claim you need to explain how a project:

- Looked for an advance in the field.
- Had to overcome the scientific or technological uncertainty.
- Tried to overcome the scientific or technological uncertainty.
- Could not be easily worked out by a professional in the field.

Your project may research or develop a new process, product or service or improve on an existing one.

HMRC are becoming more diligent in their reviews into claims being made and the rules are becoming more onerous. I recommend speaking to a specialist to ascertain whether your company is likely to have a big enough claim to warrant the work involved and then consider partnering with them to prepare and submit your claim.

Even if you are sceptical that the work you do would qualify, it is worth an hour of your time to find out for sure.

Part 3
Welcome to financial maturity

Chapter 6
Mapping strategy to figures

Financial maturity success is knowing what matters to you and having a measurable plan to get (and keep) you there – budget, management accounts and forecast.

What matters is not a destination, but a lifestyle. It is dangerous to pin all your hopes on selling your business. Firstly because only a very small percentage of businesses actually get sold, and secondly because what good is there in being miserable or desperate along the journey, just for the pot of gold at the end of the rainbow? My old mentor used the analogy of selling an hour or a car – isn't it sad that we put so much energy in at the end to tidy it up and make it look nice for the next person, when we could have been doing that all along for our own use!

I recently went on my first ski trip. They are not cheap! On my flight home I was reflecting on what a great time I had, and how fortunate I was to have been able to enjoy the experience. I was also hoping that it could become a regular activity, perhaps annually. So it's not about going on an individual ski trip, it's about affording the money and time to be able to keep going on the ski trips. If you are focused on one single event, it can be a huge anti-climax because it's over so quickly. Try to set up your business so it keeps on giving back to you.

Here are some of the threats to building a prosperous agency that not only makes good money, but is also sustainable over the long term AND gives you the freedom to step away regularly.

Client concentration

If your business generates a significant proportion of its total revenue from one or just a few individual clients, it carries the risk of falling over when that/those client(s) reduce scope or stop working with your business altogether.

If net profit margin is 20% and there is an individual client contributing 25% of the revenue, then the business is operating at a loss the moment that client disappears. Moreover, if that client is late in paying your invoices, it has a drastic impact on cash flow. Your team is more likely to overservice the bigger clients because of the impact of these risks. They operate out of fear.

You might even end up with team members being mainly or completely utilized exclusively on these bigger clients, meaning they lose exposure to other clients and therefore struggle to adapt when asked to allocate their resources elsewhere.

Lack of recurring revenue

I think it's fair to say that recurring revenue is the holy grail for every agency. The ability to bill clients month after month for broadly the same service means you can easily predict resources as well as income. You don't have to constantly re-pitch so you can allocate less resources to winning the work and more to delivering the revenue generating activities.

For this to be possible, you've got to find services that lend themselves to a repeating nature. Businesses expect to pay for some form of digital marketing over and over again because they need to keep attracting new customers. They don't expect to build a new website every month.

Agencies that offer multiple services often have a mix of recurring and project revenue for this reason. Obviously, the more that can be recurring, the stronger your business model becomes.

Woolly proposition

What do you do, who do you do it for and is that clear to the outsider?

As the number of digital agencies has increased, the requirement to 'stand out' has never been more important. Unfortunately, it had led to many agencies getting lost with their messaging. They have tried to be too clever in explaining how they are different and it just becomes confusing.

You want to make it easy for people to do business with you. Attention spans are only getting shorter so don't make your prospects have to do lots of reading to ascertain whether you provide what they need. Be bold and clear in your messaging to explain really clearly what you do and who for.

Relying on expensive talent

Great businesses need great people, but great people don't need to be expensive. Talented and experienced people will come at a premium, causing margin to be squeezed. They may come with an unwelcome ego, affecting the wider culture of the business. They are also often a significant flight risk since their experience is in demand.

Great people are those with a great attitude. They work hard, follow process and embody the values of your business. They are less expensive, easier to please and easier to replace, since they are not reliant on rare talent, but on a willingness to work with the business and its processes.

Wrong shape and size

The danger with a multi-service agency is that it relies on the right balance of opportunities landing at its door. You have a social media team, a web team and a creative team to keep busy. What's the chance of every prospect needing just the perfect balance of each of those services to align with the capacity of your agency in each of those areas? It's not going to happen.

It's key to build the size and shape of team appropriate for the revenue opportunities being presented.

Distraction

Losing focus on what the business is best at is a common issue. Owners can be guilty of allowing emotion to get in the way of delivering the plan. They get sucked into what others are doing or the gurus are saying they've lost sight of their core service.

Once you build a profit generating engine, make sure to protect and nurture and be careful not to get sidetracked by something that appears more exciting if it's only going to be a drain on resources.

Lack of process

This can be closely linked to the 'relying on expensive talent' risk above. If a business doesn't have clear processes to follow, it inevitably pays the price in the form of excess people and salaries to make up for it.

If your business is going to prosper and be enjoyable for you to run or attractive to an acquirer, it needs to have documented its way to do things. How-to guides, playbooks, Standard Operating Procedures (SOPs), whatever you want to call them, they need to be easy to follow for people with the right attitude to learn your unique *way*.

Margin erosion

It is inevitable that the costs of doing business increase over time. Salaries, rent and software rarely stay the same, so your prices mustn't either. It is understandable why businesses fear increasing their prices, but they should also fear the impacts of not increasing them.

Margin is also eroded when time spent on rechargeable work reduces. Your team's time is like diminishing stock. Once it's gone, it's gone. It cannot be recovered. The cost is incurred whether they are productive or not so you better make sure they are spending the required amount of their time on activity that generates revenue, or else you will be sinking money that you will never see again.

Appropriate investment

The appropriate investment in each area of your business, for example, marketing, office space, support staff and management, is dependent on the size and nature of the business. There is no such thing as 'best practice' because what's right for one agency is not right for another. For instance, do we need an ops manager, sales person or sophisticated customer relationship manager (CRM)? It depends on your ambition, where you are on your journey and the challenges being faced.

Chapter 7
Specialist services

MOST OF THE features of financial maturity covered so far are about cadence – doing the same things repeatedly well and making small incremental improvements over time. This consistency is really important in identifying patterns and simplifying processes without having to re-think what you're doing all the time.

There is a risk in business that when things feel too routine, we stop paying the same attention. Those behaviours are what lead to dropping standards and basic errors being made – the bane of any business owner. If you build a cadence of meetings, reporting and processes, generally the business will be simpler to run and make iterative, instead of big bang, decisions and actions.

There are, of course, times when a bigger intervention is needed, but that's even more reason to build predictability and consistency in the core operations, so that when something requires significant attention, the rest of the business doesn't fall over.

When these big decisions or projects arrive, it is important to have the right people around to support you through. Try to build a trusted network of people who are experts in their field. It might be several years before you need to call upon them but between now and then, you can assess values fit and credibility and rule them in or out as people you want to associate with.

The agencies that I have seen successfully expand overseas have typically been planning their moves for several years beforehand. They had the right people in their corner – solicitors, accountants, tax experts and other business owners who had been in their shoes. They would test their thinking on this group and take feedback on what to consider before making any costly mistakes. By the time they committed to making the move, they had significantly de-risked their decision and could execute with confidence.

Good advisers will give you some free time. They appreciate that entrepreneurs are full of ideas and if they tried to charge every time someone wanted to run their ideas by them, they would fail to build relationships. That's no good to them if the entrepreneur is ready to execute and they've taken the business to someone who would listen and truly support them on their journey.

Obviously, professional advisers can't give all of their time away for free so it's about mutual respect. Understand where the line is between discussing an idea and getting professional advice and build relationships with professionals who will be open about where that line is.

Case Study: Simon Landi

Simon Landi built a digital marketing agency specializing in enterprise level Drupal web development and sold the business 20 years after it was founded. I asked him about his experience of selling a business and working with professional advisers through the process.

What led you to implement an outsourced finance function?

We'd tried part-time employees, other outsourced finance freelancers/individuals. Nothing had quite worked and we saw the opportunity for having strategic and functional support together.

What were the key benefits that you experienced from this?

It integrated seamlessly with our processes, without bulldozing, changes were made steadily over time.

We achieved a lot more visibility. Previously we'd had very little forward visibility, or even support on what was happening in the current moment. It was only backward looking. The systems that MAP implemented absolutely gave us that. They brought a simple, but really effective financial model in and it all worked seamlessly and gave us the foresight we needed. It was revolutionary for us.

Everything before was about the last quarter and any model that was presented to us, we couldn't touch, so we couldn't pull the levers to see what effect different events were having.

We had an initial planning session which was really productive for getting everything out of our heads, and we ended up doing that every year. We were running a fast moving and dynamic businesses so we didn't often get the opportunity to sit back and look at it objectively and proactively.

Those sessions were so efficient and so much insight comes out of them. It also brings out where the gaps are, e.g. December revenue down because of Christmas and August because of holidays. We started predicting that seasonality in advance and increased our targets in other months. We were then starting to shape the business planning based on expertise that MAP has in our market. They also brought macro insights into those meetings based on what was happening in the market and in legislation, so we would be forward planning for things that we would never have planned for before.

When it came to selling your business, which services did you need to engage?

We had the ability to show the acquirer that we had well-managed finances and knew the detail. It was easy to put our hands on information and answer questions, which made the acquirer more assured.

Throughout the four-month due diligence process, the financials lined up with the forecast we'd presented to the acquirer, so we all had confidence that the value offered to buy the business wasn't going to change, because it was based on forecasted results that had now become real. The respect and trust was then there throughout.

MAP and one of my team members did all the financial due diligence, so I could focus on other aspects of the deal. I was spending 16 hours a day, 7 days a week on this and I couldn't sleep, with MAP providing out of hours support and rapid turnaround of answers which helped.

Talk us through that experience and what advice you would offer to others in similar situations

The level of detail you need, including contracts in place with customers, suppliers and team, is huge. I wish I'd involved our senior team members earlier in the process to share the burden of the work required to pull it all together.

Talk to the people who are buying you earlier in the process. You are going to be working together long term and they have sat where you are sitting so can sometimes have a more pragmatic view than the advisers.

Speak to specialists sooner. A good adviser will help you to instil the (correct) mindset to believe that you will sell the business one day, and you will therefore start to take action in order to be ready for that event.

Chapter 8
What next?

MOST PEOPLE READING this book will be owner–operators. You are a shareholder in a digital agency and you take a position either as a director on the Board or a senior employee.

As a shareholder, your goal is to make a return on your investment. Even if you haven't injected capital into the business, you will undoubtedly have injected more energy than would be expected from your role in the business. In addition, you have a lot of risk in this business as one of the biggest assets in your personal financial portfolio.

Think of it this way, the net assets on your Balance Sheet represent broadly what the business is worth in cash terms if you were to close it down after paying all the liabilities and receiving cash for all the assets. If you invested that cash into the stock market, what return would you expect? That's the minimum return you should be expecting to receive as a shareholder of the business, but in reality you should be aiming for a significantly higher return to reflect the increased risk of investing in an SME versus the safer investment of the stock market.

As a director/employee, you are responsible to deliver a role for the company that includes key decision making. You should be remunerated fairly for this role just as you should if you worked anywhere else. The great thing about being an owner–operator is that you have flexibility in the way that you extract value from the business with a combination of salary, benefits and dividends. You need to be paid well and the business needs to generate healthy profits.

Ultimately, you need to find a route to making this business a money making vehicle. That is what makes your vision and purpose possible and what gives you the financial freedom you crave for you and your family.

It doesn't come just from working harder. You need to architect the moves that get (and keep) the business where you want it to be. The P&L Report is the key management tool because it tracks what's left from deducting the expenses from the income, and in effect, the wealth generated. Cash is then regulated by executing the right financial controls to ensure that the money from the P&L flows into the business as quickly as possible.

From ego to honesty

Getting out of sales mode
Seek the weaknesses and risks
Don't be afraid to find the truth

After working with agency owners over the years, I have noticed a clear distinction between those that are running great businesses and those that struggle, and it's in the way that they see problems.

The successful owners are not only comfortable with problems but they also seek them. Business is a game full of exhilaration and challenge, highs and lows, and it's a game that we never complete. The more success you have, the more challenges you face. It's the nature of the beast. So, successful business owners are keen to find where the weaknesses and risks exist in their business before they slap them in the face. The earlier they identify them, the better the chances of tackling them before they manifest into major problems.

Those owners who spend all their time in 'sales mode' like to convince themselves and everyone they speak to that their business is flying and they seem to be getting everything right. You see them boasting on social media with their articulate posts and photos of all the wonderful things they get up to. It has become clear for me just how many of those businesses are crumbling behind the scenes. The owners live in denial about the weaknesses and risks that they face. They bury their heads in the sand and ignore the warning signs, and instead focus on keeping up appearances for that idealist brand image that they have portrayed externally.

If you can shake off the ego and be honest about the weaknesses in your business, I assure you that you will win in the long run. Nothing is that difficult given the right attention.

The curious mind

Instead of trying to convince yourself and others that you have this amazingly wonderful and perfect business, think about what questions you can be asking of the business.

This curious mind focuses on asking open questions that require a path of discovery. They are not yes/no questions and there are no right or wrong answers. It is about forcing you to uncover opportunities and mitigate risks.

For example, you might table questions such as:
- Where is it leaking money?
- Where are the opportunities to grow something that is already making a good margin?

- Where can we increase pricing?
- How can we better engage the team?
- What areas of our culture need lifting?
- How can we generate 20% more leads?
- What other markets would suit our proposition?

Clearly, this is just a small sample of the questions you could possibly table. The point is to get into the mindset of thinking of the questions or problems rather than solutions. That way you will have deeper conversations and be more considerate in coming up with the *best* solutions to the *right* problems.

Growth versus fixed mindset

I often describe this approach of seeking out and solving problems as 'the *game* of business'. It requires bravery and conviction but if you can adopt this approach, your business results will improve and life itself will be much more enjoyable.

Those with a fixed mindset restrict what they can achieve. They have already told themselves what they can and can't do and are absolute with their opinions. Those with a growth mindset are more open minded. Of course, they have opinions and beliefs but they are happy to be challenged and to seek the truth.

Instead of making knee jerk decisions, ask questions like 'how might we…', 'how do they…', 'what if…' and involve others with diverse backgrounds and opinions into group thinking. You might find yourself going around the houses a little to get to the solution, but it will be a better solution and your team will be more bought in to it.

So, let me ask you some final questions before you embark on your journey towards financial confidence:

- What does success look like for you?
- How big do you need your business to be?

- Who do you need as trusted advisers in your network?
- What cadence of meetings do you need to put in place throughout your business?
- How can you measure the value each *client* is bringing to your business?
- How can you measure the value each *team member* is bringing to your business?
- Which KPIs are most important to *your* business?
- Where can you increase prices and gain more than you lose?
- Which costs are not adding enough value?
- Which areas (services, departments, etc) have the best growth opportunities?
- Where can you easily make tax savings?
- How can you get your customers paying slightly quicker?
- When can you build recurring revenue?
- How can you improve client concentration?
- Where are the opportunities to sell your existing clients your other services?
- Who is responsible for each of the aspects of your finance function?
- Where can you delegate responsibilities to avoid you becoming a bottleneck?

We only get one shot at this life, and most of us only ever start one business. Make the most of it and make sure that first and foremost, it is focused on giving you and your family the life that you want.

For picking this book up, I thank you. For reading to the end, I am flattered. And for buying in to financial maturity to provide the platform for the business you've always wanted, I salute you!

Please do keep me posted on your progress, big or small. I would love nothing more than to hear that this book has helped you in some way.

Appendix 1
The MAP way

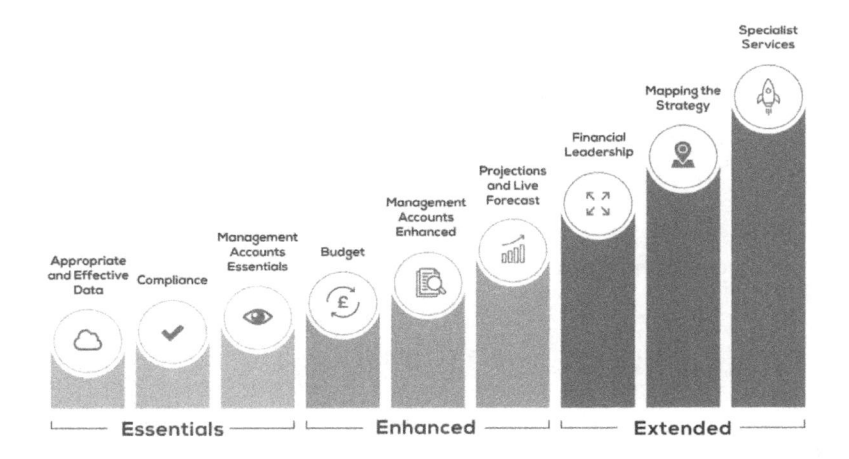

A T MAP WE manage lots of agencies at once and use that experience to learn and apply best practice.

MAP supports hundreds of digital agencies of all shapes and sizes. We love to get involved at any stage in the journey, on the proviso that you want to run your business maturely, with good financial governance and a clear plan.

Our framework helps you to diagnose where the opportunities for improvement are in the way that your business is running its finances. Together, we then implement reliable and streamlined systems to ensure that everyone is clear what needs to be done and when. We adopt the technology that we have found to be best practice for agencies like yours and we are always researching and testing on your behalf.

The finance maturity curve shows how we bring the elements of this book together to partner with agencies in their quest for financial maturity and confidence (see our resources in Appendix 2).

The first step is to book a discovery meeting. This is our opportunity to learn more about your business and see if there is a fit.

If there is an appetite to understand what working together looks like, we book a meeting to run through our proposal tool together. This approach is important because it puts you in control of the process so that we proceed with the right solution for where you are on your journey and what you need at the time.

None of the services are long-term contracts so you can adapt the solution month by month to suit your changing needs.

Should I hire an FD?

For many, the bridge between the expertise in finance and the decision-making team within the business can be underutilized. Finance can be used to prepare for change, report insights for course correction and provide the data to reward success – but it is rarely called upon to interrogate the wider business or participate in formulating strategy.

This is often a missed opportunity, and one that doesn't go unnoticed. However, the typical assumption is that the agency is now of a size and complexity that hiring an FD is the next logical step.

But is it?

You need something – but is it an FD?

Beyond keeping the finance team on track, an FD has to have a broad range of skills and business experience in order to move between the day-to-day detail, driving operational change, and the strategic work at Board level.

Typically there have been three main options that can invariably carry risk, lack value for money or leave you with a compromise in skills:

1. **In-house FD**: The problem here is that most businesses don't have the budget to invest in a full-time FD, and in the worst case scenario, fund the salary by cutting the finance function, which inevitably adds strain to getting the important basics done properly.
2. **Outsourcing an FD**: With prohibitively expensive day rates, often not enough of the right support can be brought in affordably. This also means that they are disconnected from the business or not empowered to input directly with the finance team on a day-to-day basis.
3. **Promote from within**: The other alternative has been to promote inexperienced but ambitious finance professionals who inevitably lack the necessary experience, variety and exposure to a range of industry types to add real value.

With a need for agencies to utilize a broad range of compliance, reporting and higher level skills, another way is needed. One that is affordable, results driven and builds upon what's working and in place.

A new kind of partner within the agency that is passionate about its success, investigates every part of the business and looks forward rather than just on past performance.

The finance partner

Working in tandem with both the agency and the finance function, a MAP finance partner scours the business and its activities to identify opportunities to maximize value and mitigate risk.

It's a way of raising the value of what you already have, and beyond where an FD would normally have to sit to provide the same level of effectiveness and return on investment.

A finance partner focuses on:

- Optimizing the finance function and budget (becoming an investment rather than an increased cost, often paying for themselves by reducing the overall cost of the finance function).
- Delivering direct commercial value – improving the bottom line now and sustainably into the future.
- Looking beyond the numbers to the real story – insights rather than meaningless data.
- Questioning, analyzing and supporting effective decision making – so it doesn't feel like it's all on you.

MAP clients are ahead of the game as trusting us as your finance team means that you already have quality processes and a service in place that delivers the numbers as you need them. Our finance partner allows you to elevate that service even further, without the consequences and cost of an outsourced or underpowered alternative.

Elevate your finance function

Here's a number of ways working with a finance partner can work.

Lead by design, not just opportunity

The continued success of an agency can become hard won over time. It's when you realize that things are OK, but everyone is working very hard for that OK.

In this scenario, owners know that what they have is more than a lifestyle business and are ambitious to continue to build something of real value, but don't have the capacity to work out how to get the commercial insight and analysis to make the next steps really count.

Typically, the agency has been reacting to market opportunities and demand, rather than real data. Sometimes creating financial targets and then doing whatever it takes to hit them – even if it means stretching beyond in-house expertise or reducing the profit base. The result is that they know where they are, but not how they got there.

The challenge is how to grow by design and intent, rather than gut feel and the heat of trade; in other words to:

- Optimize before growing more.
- Make decisions based on evidence and acumen.
- Refocus and prioritize commercial activity.

Expert review and a clear pathway

A finance partner brings a fresh pair of eyes to the information at hand and a new understanding of the challenges faced. Getting to know the business starts with the relationship with the senior team, the numbers and a systematic approach to uncovering whether the right questions are being asked and enough attention placed on the right things.

Covering everything from the markets served, services offered, processes employed and the type of clients targeted, a detailed audit delves into the mechanics of the business from every angle –

challenging what is known, and seeking out the hidden truths that could be used to refocus and optimize.

Working to a defined brief, the finance partner brings the design of the business back on the table, to work alongside the owner and the finance team to home in on the best use of the resource and expertise available.

An agency in a hurry

Sometimes things just click. The right product, the right time, the right team. All the crucial factors that can mean an agency accelerates from a business on the move to a business in a hurry.

Typically, these agencies are already well optimized, high performing with many processes and systems in place but the danger lies in riding the success without the proper controls – in other words, how can we continue at speed without falling off the tracks?

Investors in these businesses are more likely to be looking at how to build an asset with substantial value, usually with a future sale in mind. This approach requires a different kind of attention. Risk mitigation becomes more important than revenue opportunity, continuous improvement is sought for gains in every area and ideas for value creation are actively encouraged.

Putting value creation front and centre

Creating and consolidating value and helping to support the overall investment proposition is at the heart of how a finance partner works. Focusing on the key areas of commercial arrangements, intellectual property and risk mitigation aligns them to the potential valuation of the agency and the investors' intent.

To start, a review of the commercial contracts with clients ensures they are robust, with staged commercial terms, and assessed for risk against things like the loss of key staff and is designed to ensure the Balance Sheet is underpinned as securely as possible.

Scrutiny on intellectual property and the agency's unique sales proposition, questions what innovation is in place and how they are actually ahead of the game – usually of central importance to an acquirer who will be looking to further their competitive advantage. And tracking risks in the short, medium and long term means that key indicators like cash conversion, amounts under retainer and staff churn rate are always visible.

Monitoring the actions of the agency, working with the department heads and tracking performance by establishing metrics that are front of mind for a future buyer helps to keep the whole agency focused on building an asset rather than just growing revenue.

Definitely NOT an FD

Working so closely with digital agencies means we know that just offering a typical outsourced FD service would not be the best use of your money. However, there is a real opportunity to bring together and do so much more with the financial and non-financial information to hand.

A reliable finance function will provide quality financial control and access to reliable and timely information. Adding commercial input from an experienced finance partner elevates this service even further: someone embedded within the broader business, capable of taking a holistic view of the challenges and how they might be met.

Working with a finance partner

Inspiring our clients to partner with us at a higher level is the right thing to do when the challenges have never been tougher – and the opportunities never so rewarding.

Our finance partner brings to your agency:

- An extra injection of commercial expertise.
- A completely tailored set of objectives.
- The business skills you would expect from an FD.
- Confident input into strategy and execution.

Free consultation

For your introduction and free initial consultation with MAP, please contact me directly and I'd be delighted to arrange it: **paul@wearemap.co.uk**

Appendix 2
List of useful tools and resources

YOU MIGHT HAVE finished this book feeling somewhat overwhelmed with the amount of work needed to get your finance function operating to the level you want it.

I have created an Agency Toolkit here as a google doc with a comprehensive list of links that cover the list below and more.

https://tinyurl.com/mapagencytoolkit

As a first step, the finance maturity scorecard is designed to reduce that initial overwhelm by identifying the priority areas for you so I would recommend this being one of the first links to access.* It takes five minutes to answer the questions and get your personalized report with recommended next steps for you to take action alone or with the support of MAP.

176 | Appendix 2: List of useful tools and resources

Bonus Calculator Tool
Budgeting Template – Forecasting Templates
Capacity Planning – Profit Maximiser Tool / Capacity Working
Cash Flow Forecast (weekly view) – Forecasting Templates
*Financial Maturity Scorecard – Access Scorecard
Goal Setting Tool
Management Accounts Example
Personal Financial Planning Tool
Personal Tax Forecasting Tool (2023/24)
Take the business saleability quiz
Take the owner readiness quiz
Watch 'Profit Culture' webinar with Nikki Gatenby
Watch 'When to share a piece of the pie' webinar

Three more useful links:

Guidance on benchmark director salaries: www.payscale.com/mypayscale.aspx

Cycle Scheme Provider: www.cyclescheme.co.uk

American Express Points Rewards Card: www.americanexpress.com/uk/business/corpo-rate-cards

Note

Legislation, including tax rates and methods of calculation, are correct at the time of writing but are subject to change, so please always make sure you use the most current figures for calculations.

Appendix 3
References

1. 'Digital Marketing' first used as a term in 1990 according to Wikipedia: https://en.wikipedia.org/wiki/Digital_marketing
2. The digital transformation market is today valued in excess of $3.3 trillion: https://quixy.com/blog/top-digital-transformation-statistics-trends/#:~:text=Billion%20by%202030.-,The%20global%20digital%20transformation%20market%20is%20expected%20to%20grow%20at,from%20%24594.5%20Billion%20in%202022
3. 80% of SAAS businesses that fail in their first five years: https://pitchground.com/blog/saas-failures/#:~:text=According%20to%20a%20McKinsey%20%26%20Company%20study%2C%20only%2020%25%20of%20SaaS%20companies%20survive%20their%20first%20five%20years%20in%20business.%0A%0AThis%20underscores%20the%20importance%20of%20understanding%20the%20factors%20that%20contribute%20to%20SaaS%20company%20failure%20and%20learning%20from%20them%20to%20increase%20your%20chances%20of%20success

4. Warren Buffet calls it 'the language of business': https://smallbusiness.chron.com/accounting-referred-language-business-63107.html#:~:text=The%20Coining%20of,and%20phone%20call
5. A company will be 'small' if it has any TWO of the following: www.gov.uk/annual-accounts/microentities-small-and-dormant-companies#:~:text=Small%20companies,accounts%20to%20Companies%20House
6. According to the CCAB and CIMA, there are more than 350,000 qualified accounting professionals in the UK:
    a. www.ccab.org.uk/wp-content/uploads/2020/06/The-Accountancy-Profession-in-the-UK-and-Ireland.pdf
    b. https://committees.parliament.uk/writtenevidence/22533/pdf/#:~:text=In%20the%20UK%20alone%20CIMA,members%20working%20across%20all%20sectors

Index

accessing professional services 96
accruals concept 41–5
administration (insolvency) 38–9
advertising the business for sale 108
air miles 143
airport lounges 139
Amazon Prime subscriptions 142–3
Arden, David 82–4
assets, business 122–4
audio book subscriptions 142–3

Balance Sheet 19, 161
  buying a business 112
  cash flow forecast 65, 66
  compliance 32
  funding, securing 71, 72
  insolvency 37
  management accounting 41–2, 44–5, 55–6
  supplier payments 28
'Banker and the Fisherman' parable 87–9
bicycles and equipment 129
bonus schemes 30–1
broadband 136

Brown, Stuart 25
budget 37, 47–55, 60, 67–74
Buffett, Warren 15
Business Asset Disposal Relief 102
business class travel 138–9
business expenses paid for personally 133–43
business proposition 151
buying a business 110–14

capacity plan 51–5
capital gains tax 101–2, 117
cars 131–3, 138
  mileage claims 136–7
  parking 127–8
cash flow
  accruals concept 43, 44
  budget 50, 67–70
  buying a business 112
  forecasts 60–6, 68–70
  funding, securing 71
  insolvency 37
  management accounts 56–7
  value of the business 104
  VAT payments 31
certainty, securing 105

Index

childcare 128–9
clients
   best and worst 92–5
   concentration 57, 150
closing a business 39
cloud accounting 23, 28, 29
commercial health check 57–9
commuting costs 137–40
Companies House 29–30, 32, 33, 37, 40, 97
company voluntary arrangement (CVA) 38
compensation to revenue 58
compliance 29–31
compulsory liquidation 39
confidence 18–19
confirmation statement 33
congestion charge 137
continue option 8–10
corporation tax *see* taxation
cost reviews 28–9
creches 129
credit control 27–8, 62–3
creditors' voluntary liquidation (CVL) 39
credit scores 96–8, 104
   after insolvency 40
   compliance 29
   funding, securing 73
   salaries 115
critical illness cover 131
culture, organizational 78–9
curiosity 163–4
current assets and liabilities 64–6
current ratio 66
cycle schemes 129

data, appropriate and effective 26–9
dates, key 31–5
debt finance 72
default, building an agency by 95

deferred consideration 111–12
dentistry costs 130
design, building an agency by 95–6
directors
   funding, securing 72, 74
   insolvency 37–41
   salaries 89
director's ban 40–1
director's loan account 65, 134
distraction 152
dividends 116–17
double entry system 44–5
Downes, Adam 85–6
due diligence 108, 112–13, 114, 158

earnout 112
education fees 143–5
electric vehicles 132–3
employee benefits 120–1, 125–33
employment allowance 115, 116
employment packages 30
entertaining costs 141–2
Entrepreneurs Relief 102
equity 71–2, 99–100
errors 29
exiting the business 8, 106–10
experience, finance partners 78

family members
   education fees 143–5
   employing 116, 127
   gifts 127
   investment companies 117
   shares 117
finance, securing 70–4, 96–7, 111–12
financial leadership 76–84
financial maturity curve 23–4
   enhanced 47–74
   essentials 25–45
   extended 75–145
financial performance versus financial maturity 19–21

Index | 181

first-class travel 138–9
Fish, Jimmy 36–41
fixed mindset 164
focus, loss of 152
forecasts 59–66, 68–71
freelancers 58
funding, securing 70–4, 96–7, 111–12

Gatenby, Nikki 57–9
gifts 126–7
glass ceiling 14–16, 48
goal setting tool 89–91
gross margin 90
growth mindset 164–5
growth shares 102–3
gyms 129–30

HMRC
  compliance 29, 33
  share options 101–2
  taking money out of the
    company 121, 124, 136,
    141–2, 144–5
home working expenses 135–6
honesty 163

incident overnight expenditure 141
income protection insurance 131
inheritance tax 123
insolvency 35–41
intellectual property 106, 111
interest payments 120–1
investment, appropriate 153
invoices 27, 28, 63

Jarvis, Will 45

Key Performance Indicators (KPIs)
  51, 55, 57

Landi, Simon 156–9
late night working costs 137–8

lawyers 109, 113
life insurance 125
lifestyle business 87–9, 149–50
liquidation 39
loans 96–7, 119–22
lose–lose clients 93, 94
lose–win clients 92, 93–4
lunches 128

management accounts 41–5, 55–9
MAP 23–4, 95–8, 107–8, 157–8,
  167–74
margin erosion 153
medical insurance 130
mileage claims 136–7
misfeasance 40
mobile phones 126
money needs 85–6
music subscriptions 142–3

national insurance 101, 114–16,
  118–19, 129, 132, 134–5,
  142–3

optician costs 130
overheads
  goal setting tool 90
  months of cover 58
  projections 59, 66
  reviews 28–9
overnight expenditure 141

PAYE 31
payroll 29, 30, 31
pensions 117–19
  advice 125–6
  compliance 29, 30, 31–2
  contributions 117
  State Pension 114, 115
pipeline value 58
points rewards cards 143
prepayments 65

process, lack of 152–3
profile of the business 105–6
Profit & Loss (P&L) Report 19, 162
  compliance 33
  funding, securing 71
  goal setting tool 91
  management accounting 41–2, 44–5, 55–6
  supplier payments 28
profits
  accruals concept 43–4
  bonus schemes 30–1
  budget 50, 51, 53, 54
  commercial health check 57
  projections 60
  retained 90
  value exchange 91–2
  value of the business 104
projections 59–66, 68–71
public transport 138, 139

qualifications, finance partners 77–8

referrals for lose–lose clients 94–5
rent 122–3
research and development 115, 145
revenue
  capacity plan 52, 53
  commercial health check 57, 58
  projections 59, 60
  recognition 41–5
  recurring 150–1
risk removal/mitigation
  buying a business 111, 112–14
  value of the business 105

salaries 114–15
scaling the business 98–103, 110–11
self-assessment 33–5

selling the business 8, 39, 106–10, 158
shareholder protection insurance 131
shareholder returns 90
shares 99–103, 117
size of market 3
snacks 128
Software as a Service (SAAS) businesses 5–6
specialist services 96–114, 155–9
spouse 116, 117
startup stage 16–17
statutory requirements, compliance with 29–31
stop option 8
strategy, mapping the 84–96
struggling businesses 7–8
  accruals concept 43–4
  finance partners 80–1
  insolvency 35–41
subscriptions 142–3
subsistence 140–1
supplier payments 28
systemizing the business 104–5

taking money and value out of the company 114–45
talent 151–2
taxation
  business expenses paid for personally 116–38, 141–5
  compliance 29, 31, 33–5
  employment packages 30
  non-payment 40
  pension contributions 30
  share options 101–2
  taking money out of the company 115, 118–19, 125, 128, 132–4, 142, 145
taxis 137–8, 139
team size and shape 152

training 128
travel 137–40
trivial benefits 126–7
TUPE regulations 39

utilization 58

value exchange 91–2
   value of the business 104–6

VAT 128, 132, 141, 142
   compliance 29, 31

win–lose clients 93
win–win clients 92, 93
working capital 64, 66

year-end accounts 32